C000263250

The Way to Wear'em

BY THE SAME AUTHOR

(with Vanda Foster) Crinolines and Crimping Irons: *Victorian Clothes – How They Were Cleaned and Cared For*

The Ghost in the Looking Glass: *The Victorian Seamstress*

The Way to Wear'em

150 Years of **Punch** on Fashion

Christina Walkley

Peter Owen · London

ISBN 0 7206 0627 6

All Rights Reserved. No part of this publication
may be reproduced in any form or by any means
without the prior permission of the publishers.

Designed by Frances McKay

PETER OWEN PUBLISHERS
73 Kenway Road London SW5 0RE

First published 1985
© Christina Walkley 1985

Printed in Great Britain by
Photobooks (Bristol) Ltd

To Oliver

Acknowledgements

Permission to use quoted material included in this book has been granted by courtesy of the following:

Curtis Brown Ltd, on behalf of Daphne du Maurier, for an extract from *Rebecca*, copyright 1938 Daphne du Maurier;

Faber & Faber Ltd for extracts from *Period Piece* by Gwen Raverat;

Hamish Hamilton Ltd for extracts from *Edwardian Daughters* by Sonia Keppel;

Lutterworth Press for an extract from *Little Town on the Prairie* by Laura Ingalls Wilder;

Macdonald & Co. (Publishers) Ltd for an extract from *Cap and Bell* by Susan and Asa Briggs;

Octopus Books Ltd for an extract from *Dior in Vogue* by Brigid Keenan;

Oxford University Press for an extract from *Lark Rise to Candleford* by Flora Thompson;

A.D. Peters & Co. Ltd for an extract from *Two Flamboyant Fathers* by Nicolette Devas, published by William Collins Sons & Co. Ltd;

Laurence Pollinger Ltd for an extract from *A Girl Like I* by Anita Loos. Proprietors: Viking Penguin, Inc.

Many people have helped with the writing of this book. First I want to thank the Editor of *Punch* for allowing me to reproduce material still in copyright, and Ms Mary Anne Bonney, *Punch*'s Librarian, for her help and co-operation. My husband Phill has given me immeasurable support and encouragement throughout the project, as well as endlessly carrying heavy volumes to and fro and being an indefatigable photocopier. My sister Genevieve gave me hospitality during one of my research periods; Carolyn Waterfall and Angela Hamm have been generous baby-sitters; Simon Mauger kindly lent me his collection of *Punch* and Kevin Howlett gave me the answers to some obscure queries. Finally the staff at Street Library have been unfailingly helpful and accommodating. To all of them I am deeply grateful.

C.W.

Contents

Note

Punch is collected into six-monthly volumes. From 14 July 1855 onwards, the contents of each volume are subdivided into weeks, each with its own date; but until that time, that is to say for the first twenty-eight volumes, there are no internal dates at all. When giving references for quotations, therefore, the following system has been adopted. Any material before the middle of 1855 is identified by the half-year and the page number – for example, II, 1849, p. 113; while anything after that time carries the date of the particular number it appeared in – for example, 14 September 1878.

Introduction

Clothes, whether they are regarded as examples of decorative art or as mere domestic artefacts, are unique in that they posit a creative relationship between them and their wearer. The same dress on two different people is no longer the same dress. Clothes can affect a person's posture, behaviour, self-image and, ultimately, social status; but equally the wearer can infuse a garment with his or her personality and transform it. The successful fashion model can endow the most mediocre dress with some of her own magnetism. A dress on a hanger means little: we need to understand its context, its implications, the influences that went to shape it, its effects. Students of costume must seek their information from the greatest variety of sources – pictorial, literary, historical, psychological. Cartoons are an exceptionally good source, and for anyone who is looking for a sustained vade-mecum to fashion over the last 140 years, *Punch* is without parallel.

The *Punch* that was first launched upon the English scene in July 1841 was very different from *Punch* today. In its very first paragraph it made the point that, although its title might suggest 'no other intention than the amusement of a thoughtless crowd', it had a more serious purpose as well. It was socially and politically radical, and in the England of 1841, a country that was depressed, hungry and divided, it had plenty to be radical about. Most of the staff were young; many, like Mayhew and Thackeray, were brilliant and later famous; and under the inspired editorship of Mark Lemon they produced a fundamentally humorous but hard-hitting publication not unlike today's *Private Eye*.

However, despite its radical outlook, there were ways in which *Punch* was deeply conservative. It was written by London men for London men: the provinces existed only as a subject for jokes, either about the trials of Londoners who ventured into the country, or about the absurdity of provincials who came up to London. Abroad was unspeakable, and women were a joke. Admittedly *Punch* was willing and eager to champion exploited womanhood in the form of overworked seamstresses or governesses, but only while they did not attempt to champion themselves. 'Unexploited' women, such as the wives and daughters of the readership, were fair game. Doubtless a racier publication would have jibed at 'the sex' with more frank contempt. But *Punch*, although written for men, was intended to be read by the whole family and contented itself with being patronizing, rising to open hostility only when dealing with 'strong-minded' women, whom it invariably depicted with sharp noses, stringy hair and glasses.

By the early 1860s *Punch* had lost much of its revolutionary fervour. There had been changes in the staff, and changes too in the country. As Asa Briggs remarks in the introduction to his anthology *Cap and Bell*:

> By 1861, when *Punch* celebrated its twentieth birthday, the mood of the country was so mellow that it was difficult to arouse any sustained interest in further political reform. There were few outspoken radical critics, and most commentators on society dwelt not on its tensions but on its harmonies, not on its conflicts but on its conformities. Above all, they concerned themselves with the implications of its unprecedented rate of material progress.

In addition to this, *Punch*'s outspokenness had been somewhat shaken by the sudden death of the Prince Consort, who for years had been a regular target for savage criticism. In death he became instantly inviolate; *Punch* had to produce a hasty and manifestly insincere lament for his loss and thereafter became more cautious. Thus *Punch* grew respectable. It ceased to be primarily a righter of wrongs and a champion of the oppressed (although it maintained an interest in 'causes' at least till the end of the century), and became instead a chronicle of metropolitan life. The fashionable world was now its sphere; from Leech's pictures of cockney life we move to George du Maurier and the drawing-room.

Almost from the beginning, feminine love of finery had been satirized in *Punch*, but the 1840s were not a fertile time for costume jokes. The depressed state of the country was reflected in its fashions. The great age of the dandies was over and men were resigning themselves to the colourless, unimaginative clothes with which they have been cursed ever since, while women, too, adopted muted colours and restrained shapes, in sharp contrast to the wild flights of fancy of the 1820s and 1830s. By the late 1850s and early 1860s, however, Britain's economic expansion had led to a renewed enthusiasm in fashion and a rapidly increasing market for it. Crinolines, striped stockings and aniline dyes were just a few manifestations of this new self-confidence. The introduction of a rapid succession of styles and their almost universal adoption, facts which we take for granted today but which were a startling novelty then, meant that fashion became a subject for satire in its own right, and costume jokes and cartoons proliferated, making *Punch* an invaluable record for the costume historian.

Despite fashion's endless vagaries the basic repertoire of the humorist is limited, and it is interesting to see how, over a period of several decades, the same idea may recur as the kernel of a joke, though the details and the treatment are different. In Chapter 6 we shall see how du Maurier repeated, at a twenty-year interval, his joke about young women in 'masculine' attire being mistaken for youths and thus giving offence by keeping their hats on in church; and the cartoon of 1899 (Plate 112), which gives this book its title, reappeared nearly forty years later (Plate 122), with a shift from knickerbockers to shorts and a marked change of style. The earlier version, by Partridge, is one of those familiar *Punch* cartoons which combine a wealth of detail with a total disregard for pithiness, while Fougasse, in 1936, has pared down both drawing and

1 *1 June 1867*

2 *25 March 1871*

A REMARKABLE STUDY FROM NATURE.

"THE BURDENS OF FASHION."

WHAT WE MUST COME TO BEFORE LONG!

caption to a minimum which none the less says it all. Here, and constantly in the pages of *Punch*, the essential humour is not a question of the clothes themselves, but of usage and social context – the way to wear 'em.

During the rest of its history *Punch* has naturally undergone many changes in outlook and format, but it has not substantially shifted from its solid, middle-class, London-based standpoint. Moreover, it has retained no more political content than has been necessary to keep it topical. It has been witty and entertaining, but seldom outrageous; it has reflected changing social attitudes, but rarely shaped them. When, in the late 1920s, it increased substantially in size, much of the extra space was devoted to book, theatre and film reviews. However, in much more recent years there has been a conscious attempt to make the cover more immediately topical and to break away from the dentist's waiting-room image.

The years between the wars were the last great period of costume jokes, as female legs were alternately displayed to the world or encased in trousers, make-up became an everyday sight and dieting a common obsession, and even men allowed themselves the frivolity of Oxford bags and Fair Isle jumpers. But war and austerity overcame this exuberance, and in the post-war world the gradual emancipation of women and the erosion of class differences have rendered much of the traditional humour about costume unacceptable, at least to the sort of people who read *Punch*. Jokes about dress are scarce in the 1940s and 1950s, and by the 1960s and 1970s even miniskirts and platform shoes provoke little laughter. Tolerance and broadmindedness about personal eccentricity have become the favourite virtues of the informed middle class, and they do not provide a fertile ground for caricature.

The first inestimable advantage of cartoons over other forms of costume illustration is that here, as nowhere else, it is possible to see a fashion at its worst. Paintings, fashion plates and photographs all seek to flatter their subject and show it at its most attractive, immobilized in a moment of perfection. (Casual snapshots, which often capture their subject in an unfortunate pose, are an exception, but in the Victorian period at least they were very rare: most photographs were elaborately posed.) The cartoon, being facetious, does the exact opposite, but is no less truthful in its way. How else would we know how crinolines behaved in a high wind? (See, for example, Plates 1, 2 and 3, progressing from strict observation to comic fantasy.) Of course the cartoon exaggerates, to the

SKETCH ON THE SEA COAST DURING THE GALE.

Lord D—ndre—ry (to his Brother). "A-A-A, I THAY, THAM ! WATHER A DITHPLAY OF FIGGER—EH !"

3   *16 August 1862*

4   *6 October 1866*

CONVOLVULUS SEASIDEIENSIS.

"THIS DELICATE ANNUAL HAS BEEN SEEN IN GREAT ABUNDANCE THIS AUTUMN ALL ROUND THE COAST. IT FLOURISHES BEST IN EXPOSED SITUATIONS, AND DURING INCLEMENT, WINDY WEATHER."—*Vide "Jolly Gardeners' Chronicle."*

A SKETCH DURING THE RECENT GALE.

5 *20 December 1856*

same degree as the fashion plate, though in an opposite direction. No beauty of the 1820s had quite such sloe eyes or india-rubber shoulders as Alais's drawings, and the women of the 1890s strove in vain to reduce their waists to fashion-plate smallness. Similarly no skirt of the late 1860s was as long as du Maurier would have us believe (Plate 4), nor were the false chignons of the 1870s as burdensome as Plate 5 suggests; but in both cases the essential truth can be easily divined and the exaggeration enjoyed on its own level. The facetious nature of cartoons also means that subjects like underwear can be touched on, albeit delicately, at a time when they would have been thought questionable in any other context (Plate 6).

Cartoons are frequently little cameos of daily life, illustrating behaviour and manners as much as appearance. We see not merely a crinoline, but one trying to board a bus, and incidentally we gauge other people's reactions to it; Oxford bags, not in repose, but trying to cross a muddy street. In cartoons we can appreciate the delicate shades of snobbery associated with dress and understand not just which style was prevalent in a particular season, but how quickly the servants adopted it and just how much resentment this caused among their mistresses. We see references to the cost of dress, both in money and in human effort. We gain insights into the battle of the sexes. In short, cartoons can record not just the fashion itself, but all its social, economic, political and

Dreadful Boy. "MY EYE, TOMMY, IF I CAN'T SEE THE OLD GAL'S LEGS THROUGH THE PEEP HOLES!"

6   *24 July 1858*

AN AFFAIR OF IMPORTANCE.

Harriet. "OH! I'M SO GLAD YOU ARE COME, BLANCHE! I HAVE BEEN SO
PERPLEXED I COULD HARDLY SLEEP ALL NIGHT."
Blanche. "WELL! WHAT IS IT, DEAR!"
Harriet. "WHY, I DON'T KNOW WHETHER TO HAVE MY NEW MERINO
FROCK VIOLET OR DARK BLUE!"

7   *II, 1852, p. 270*

FOR BACHELORS THINKING OF MARRIAGE.

Mrs. Jones. " O, MALCOLM, LOOK ! THAT'S THE VERY MRS. BROWN WE MET AT THE ROBINSONS' LAST WEEK ! I SHOULD LIKE
TO SINK INTO THE EARTH ! ! "

Mr. Jones. " WHY, DEAREST ? WHY ? "

Mrs. Jones. " O, MALCOLM, JUST THINK ! I WORE THE SAME DRESS I 'VE GOT ON TO-NIGHT ! "

8   *30 March 1872*

psychological implications.

Not being a fashion magazine as such, *Punch* is never committed to
recording dress simply because it is fashionable; the initial impulse lies
elsewhere, in the artist's whim or fancy. He may choose, then, to give
undue prominence (undue, that is, from a costume historian's point of
view) to some extreme fashion which was worn only by a minority, while
neglecting to record some other style, universally worn yet somehow
failing to fire his imagination. Bloomers are the most obvious example of
a fashion which had minimal impact in terms of actual wearers but was
given such extensive coverage in *Punch* that one might suppose every girl
in England wore them. An interesting contrast is provided by the bustle
of the 1880s, an artificial structure utterly at variance with the natural
curves of the female body, and which made sitting down almost
impossible, but which was, inexplicably, almost totally ignored by the
cartoonists of the period.

To warrant inclusion in *Punch*, then, a garment or mode had to be
potentially funny as well as just fashionable. It could qualify on many
different counts. In the early years of *Punch* the very idea of fashion
seemed inexpressibly funny: this was because it was both feminine and
foreign. While it seemed quite right and natural to Victorian man to

Dumpy Young Lady. " WELL, FOR MY PART, MATILDA, I LIKE LONG
WAISTS AND FLOUNCES."

9   *II, 1846, p. 52*

deny his wife and daughters any useful occupation, he nevertheless
found their interest in clothes hilariously funny (Plates 7 and 8).
Incapable and unwilling as he was to understand the logistics of fashion,
he thought that women voluntarily enslaved themselves to an exacting
and capricious tyrant in the mistaken belief that this would make them
attractive – further proof, if any were needed, of their total mindlessness:

> Young gentlemen of England,
>   That only mind your ease,
> Ah, little do you think how hard
>   Young ladies try to please!
> Give ear unto the Milliners,
>   And they will plainly show
> How the waist must be laced,
>   By the Fashion-books to go.
>
> She who'd attract attention
>   Must laugh at common sense,
> For when one goes to choose a dress,
>   One mustn't mind expense;
> Nor think how Pa will scold one,
>   Whene'er he comes to know
> How he's let into debt,
>   By the Fashion-books to go.

> What terrible privations
>   Young ladies must endure,
> A lovely face and form of grace
>   From damage to secure!
> Their appetites they must control,
>   Lest they too stout should grow,
> And in vain strive and strain,
>   By the Fashion-books to go.
>
> In days of bitter weather,
>   Which winter doth enforce,
> One cannot think of such a thing
>   As good thick boots, of course;
> With instep undefended,
>   In rain, and hail, and snow,
> All so bold one gets cold,
>   By the Fashion-books to go.

II, 1844, p. 260

To add insult to injury, the despotic power which held the paterfamilias's womenfolk in thrall did not even originate in Britain, but in France. The language of fashion borrowed heavily from French, and articles about dress were larded with italicized words incomprehensible to an outsider. During the 1840s *Punch* amused its male readers with parodies of these:

Dimity boas are now quite in fashion. Gowns should be of the elegant shape called *trousseaux*, or looped with *attachè*. Ladies moving in the highest circles are not unfrequently seen in bonnets of *rechauffé* trimmed with corduroy to match. A light scarf of *quilted crenoline*, or a shawl lined with *artiste* or *coupè*, gives a graceful finish to a good figure. *Coup d'oeil* is not so much in vogue for muffs; but those made of *blasé*, are beginning to be the rage. Parasols, to be in the highest fashion, should be of *bombazine a la récherché*, but we have noticed a few of the beautiful fabric *carte blanche*.

I, 1848, p. 91

As time went on, the mere existence of fashion as a phenomenon ceased to be considered funny, and extracts from fashion magazines, whether straight quotations or parodies, were not sufficient to amuse. But women's obedience to the mode still formed the gist of many jokes, especially when they adopted unbecoming clothes simply because they were fashionable (Plates 9 and 10). *Punch*, however, reflected contemporary social attitudes, and, while deploring slavish obedience to the fashion of the day, recognized that outright rejection of it simply looked ludicrous (Plates 11 and 12).

Until women had gained a measure of economic independence, their extravagance in dress was a subject close to the male heart. Dress in Victorian times was expensive in comparison with other commodities, and *Punch* is full of barely facetious complaints about it:

> Heaven gave us Lovely Woman, and the devil gave her fashion books! This would many a man be tempted to exclaim, when pulling a long face at the long bill which his wife wants him to pay for her adornment. . . . Dear creatures as they are, in a sumptuary sense, ladies would be even dearer, in a right sense, to their husbands, if they would be a trifle cheaper in matters of costume. With beef at twenty pence a pound (which seems probable ere Christmas) extravagance in dress must lead in many houses to

10   *6 November 1929*

Modiste. "IT IS, AS MADAM SAYS, CLOSE-FITTING; BUT MADAM MUST REMEMBER THAT IT IS ONLY THUS THAT SHE CAN ACHIEVE THE 'MERMAID LINE' WHICH IS SO ESSENTIAL FOR THE PRESENT MODE."

MORE NOVELTY.

The Misses Weasel think Crinoline a preposterous and extravagant invention, and appear at Mrs. Roundabout's Party in a Simple and Elegant Attire.

11 *21 November 1857*   12 *4 March 1893*

HISTORY CONTRADICTS ITSELF.

The Misses Roundabout think Tight Skirts a preposterous and extravagant Invention, and appear at Mrs. Weasel's Party in a Simple and Elegant Attire.   [*Vide "Punch" for Nov. 21, 1857.*

"Really, my dear, every time I look at that new hat of yours I can't help laughing."
"Can't you? Then I'll put it on when the bill arrives."

13 *28 March 1928*

short commons in the larder. . . . To people with short purses, fine clothing means cold mutton; and now mutton is so dear, it may shortly mean *soup maigre*, and well nigh prison fare. Husbands, whose finances are somewhat in low water must all turn vegetarians, if the price of meat increases, unless their wives submit to some diminishment in dress.

19 August 1865

Hats became the most potent symbol of vanity and extravagance (Plate 13), so for years afterwards, indeed until hats went out of fashion, the arrival of the milliner's bill or the return home of a wife laden with hat boxes formed the subject of innumerable jokes.

Dress has always been used to express real or fancied social distinctions, and *Punch* was well aware of how a snobbish and sought-after dressmaker could put her clients in their place (Plate 14). Its strongest condemnation, however, was reserved for women, servants or otherwise, who tried to dress above their station (Plate 15).

Because a preoccupation with dress was held to be an essentially female characteristic, *Punch* was very ready to ridicule any male who so far forgot his manhood as to care deeply about his appearance (Plates 16 and 17), and for a long time a feeling subsisted that women were alienated and disgusted by dandies.

AT MADAME ALDEGOND'S (REGENT STREET).

First Dressmaker. "Do you—a—wear Chamois Leather Underclothing?"
New Customer. "No; certainly not."
First Dressmaker. "Oh! then pray take a Seat, and I will send the *Second* Dressmaker!"

14   *19 April 1879*   15   *27 January 1904*

"SLUM UP-TO-DATE."

Polly (to District Visitor). "Please, Miss, Mother says she's not 'at 'ome' to-day. You see she's trimmin' her 'at to go to a Party"

My hat displayed a glossy sheen,
  My coat was trimly planned
The day I sought Evangeline
  And offered her my hand;
I wore the latest fancy vest,
  The smartest boots in Town,
And much I marvelled what possessed
  The girl to turn me down.

With hopes extinguished by a blight,
  I lost my mental peace,
A portion of my appetite
  And all my centre-crease;
I fell away in dull despair
  From true sartorial grace;
The pattern of my pedal-wear
  Grew almost commonplace.

I showed in my excessive grief
  To every passer-by
A glimpse of pocket-handkerchief
  That failed to match my tie;
The dandy that I used to be
  So disappeared from view
That people might have taken me
  For any one of you.

Till, as I went my moody way
  And flaunted in the street
An undistinguished *négligé*,
  Once more we chanced to meet,
And, when I thought she'd eye askance
  My toilet drab and plain,
I saw a something in her glance
  That bade me try again.

And jocund soon became my mien,
  My cares were cast behind
The day I gave Evangeline
  A chance to change her mind;
Devoid of gloves and spatless, I
  Had so increased my charms,
She heaved an acquiescent sigh
  And fell into my arms.

14 February 1923

If men were supposed to be manly, women were certainly expected to be feminine, and one of *Punch*'s first sustained outbursts was against the fashion for bloomers. In this case a style of dress was ridiculed quite savagely, not because it was in itself ludicrous, but because it was the visible expression of the thing Victorian man most dreaded: woman asserting herself. Thus the pictures which appeared in *Punch* bore very little relation to what 'Bloomerites' actually looked like, but they are extraordinarily revealing of contemporary male fears (Plate 18).

Of course *Punch* did not aim its satire only at the wearers of fashion: some styles or garments were potentially funny regardless of who wore them or why. It may have been that they subjected the wearer to laughable mishaps – crinolines were a particular case in point (Plate 19); or that they unwittingly invited unflattering comparisons with less exalted modes of dress (Plate 20); or that their shape led the cartoonist to a comical association of ideas (Plate 21).

And sometimes, instead of ridiculing a particular fashion, *Punch* simply allowed itself a good laugh about the whole process (Plate 22):

First Cock Sparrow. "WHAT A MIWACKULOUS TYE, FWANK. HOW THE D[ ] DO YOU MANAGE IT!"
Second Cock Sparrow. "YAS. I FANCY IT IS RATHER GRAND; BUT THEN, [ ] SEE, I GIVE THE WHOLE OF MY MIND TO IT!"

16   *II, 1853, p. 18*

THE HEIGHT OF MASHERDOM.

' WELL, TA-TA OLD MAN! MY PEOPLE ARE WAITING UP FOR
ME, YOU KNOW!"   "WHY, DON'T YOU CARRY A LATCH-KEY?"
"CARRY A *LATCH-KEY!* NOT I! A LATCH-KEY 'D SPOIL *ANY*
FELLER'S FIGURE!"

17   *4 February 1888*

18   *II, 1851, pp. 204–5*

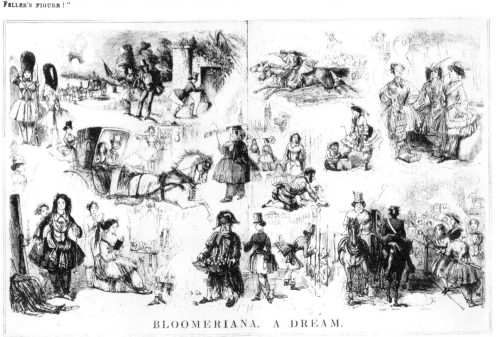

BLOOMERIANA. A DREAM.

OLD LADY (wrathfully, but with dignity, to the Constable's scandalous suggestion). "*It's nothing of the kind, P'liceman, that I can assure you; but I have unfortunately entangled my foot in my Crinoline, and can't get it out!*"

19   *20 June 1863*

There was a time when girls wore hoops of steel,
   And with grey powder used to drug their hair,
Bedaubed their cheeks with rouge: white lead, or meal,
   Adding, to simulate complexions fair:
Whereof by contrast to enhance the grace,
Specks of court-plaister decked the female face.

That fashion passed away, and then were worn
   Dresses whose skirts came scarce below the knee,
With waists girt round the shoulder-blades, and Scorn
   Now pointed at the prior finery,
When here and there some antiquated dame
Still wore it, to afford her juniors game.

Short waists departed; Taste awhile prevailed;
   Till ugly Folly's reign returned once more,
And ladies then again went draggle-tailed;
   And now they wear hoops also, as before.
Paint, powder, patches, nasty and absurd,
They'd wear as well, if France but spoke the word.

UNCONSCIOUS PLAGIARISM.

A Case of "Mimicry" in Natural History recently observed in the London streets.

20 *6 January 1909*

MIGHT NOT THE PRESENT PANNIER DRESSES BE MADE USEFUL AS WELL AS ORNAMENTAL?

21 *4 September 1869*

22 *17 August 1867*

PERHAPS.

Stout Fashionable Party. "WHAT GUYS THEY MADE OF THEMSELVES IN THOSE DAYS, AUNT!"
Slim Old Ditto. "FASHION, MY DEAR! I SHOULD NOT WONDER BUT *WE* SHALL BE LOOKED ON AS *PERFECT FRIGHTS* IN FUTURE TIMES!!"

Young bucks and beauties, ye who now deride
    The reasonable dress of other days;
When Time your forms shall have puffed out or dried,
    Then on your present portraits youth will gaze,
And say what dowdies, frights, and guys you were,
With their more specious figures to compare.

Think, if you live till you are lean or fat,
    Your features blurred, your eyes bedimmed with age,
Your limbs have stiffened; feet grown broad and flat;
    You may see other garments all the rage,
Preposterous as even that attire
Which you in full-length mirrors now admire.

16 June 1860

1 Domestic Bliss

The solid comfort of Victorian middle-class life could not have existed for one moment without the vast army of servants which underpinned it. In an age of boundless social ambition and cheap labour, the smallest household with any pretensions to gentility kept two or three servants; partly, it is true, because there was often simply too much housework for one pair of hands, but also because it was considered vulgar to open the front door oneself, to cook one's own meals or look after one's children.

Servants and masters existed in a kind of symbiosis, the servants dependent on their masters for economic survival and the masters no less dependent on their servants for physical survival. They often lived on terms of the greatest intimacy: butlers and nannies, certainly ladies'-maids and gentlemen's valets, while all belonging to what was considered a decidedly inferior class, occupied positions of great trust and might know every detail of their masters' private lives. But about their own lives they were expected to display an unobtrusiveness bordering on self-annihilation. We have only to think of Paul Dombey's wet-nurse Polly Toodle, who not only had to renounce her own family for the duration of her contract, but was required to change her name to Richards; or of the surprise with which Soames Forsyte learnt, after years of familiarity, that the family butler was married. And servants were expected to be as reticent in the indulgence of their tastes in dress as they were about their personal relationships.

It was, and always had been, accepted that personal servants received as perks their employers' cast-off clothing (Plate 23). Indeed in the eighteenth century this was one of the only ways in which fashion could disseminate itself. When Pamela's mistress died, the master shared out the clothing between her servants. This much was considered right and proper, but if the servants were suspected of inordinate vanity, or of ideas above their station, they quickly became objects of ridicule (Plates 24 and 25). Such was the fate of Humphry Clinker and his sweetheart

"CHACUN POUR SOI."

Lady's-Maid. "I BEG PARDON, MA'AM, BUT YOUR DRESS IS TRAILING—HADN'T I BETTER LOOP IT UP BEFORE YOU GO OUT?"
Lady. "No, THANKS, PARKER, I PREFER LETTING IT TRAIL, AS IT'S THE FASHION JUST NOW—"
Lady's-Maid. "YES, MA'AM—BUT AS THE DRESS IS TO BE *MINE* SOME DAY, I THINK *I* OUGHT TO HAVE SOME SAY IN THE MATTER!"

SERVANTGALISM;
OR, WHAT'S TO BECOME OF THE MISSUSES?—No. 3.

Old Lady. "WHAT IS IT, BOY?"
Boy. "PLEASE 'M—IT'S A PAIR OF WHITE SATING SHOES, AND THE LADY'S FAN WOT'S BIN MENDED—NAME OF MISS JULIER PEARLASH!"
Old Lady. "MISS!!!???????!"
Voice from Area. "OH, IT'S ALL RIGHT, MUM. IT'S ME!"

23   *4 November 1876*

24   *I, 1853, p. 118*

Win, who dressed themseves up rather too flashily in their hand-me-downs and were hooted at in the street. And yet a lady's-maid's passionate interest in dress was not just a foible: she was, after all, professionally involved as well. It was part of a parlourmaid's statutory duties to do the household needlework in the afternoons and, if no lady's-maid was kept, she had to help her mistress to dress, keep her wardrobe in order and look after the fine linens. A lady's-maid was even more concerned with clothes, having to dress and undress her mistress, put out her clothes for walking, riding, driving and the evening, wash her lace and fine linen (itself a specialized task), and keep her wardrobe in thorough repair, as well as undertaking dressmaking and millinery. Sonia Keppel remembered that, in 1914,

. . . one of the facts of war that had most impressed me had been Mamma's ability suddenly to do without Miss Draper, and to go off to Etaples with only a small suitcase as her luggage. Now, I recalled the daily services that Miss Draper had always done for Mamma: drawing her bath and scenting it with rose-geranium bath salts; setting out her underclothes under their lace cover; kneeling on the floor to put on Mamma's stockings, lacing Mamma into her stays (as though she were reining in a runaway horse); doing her hair; pinning her veil on to her hat; buttoning up her gloves; putting her powder and cigarettes and money into her bag. And, behind the scenes, washing, ironing, mending. It had quite worried me to think of Mamma bereft of all this help.

Many lady's-maids were indeed trained dressmakers, who could not stand the gruelling pace of work in a fashion house but found the experience they had gained invaluable. Thus they were women who knew and understood dress and fashion, yet their interest was supposed to remain academic. Occasionally then a maid with a highly developed sense of style might feel frustrated and affronted if her mistress failed to live up to it (Plate 26). Daphne du Maurier's luckless Mrs de Winter found herself in this situation:

25　*17 March 1877*

FASHIONS FOR THE KITCHEN.

Cook. "Lor', Jane, I wouldn't be bothered with them 'Trains' every Day! I only wears mine on Sundays!"

Jane. "That may do for *you*, Cook; but for my part I likes to be a Lady Week-Days as *well* as Sundays!"

The housemaid Alice had been so superior. I used to sneak my chemise and nightgowns out of my drawer and mend them myself rather than ask her to do them. I had seen her once, with one of my chemises over her arm, examining the plain material with its small edging of lace. I shall never forget her expression. She looked almost shocked, as though her own personal pride had received a blow.

While they were on duty, servants wore uniform. A parlourmaid, for example, wore a print gown with apron and cap in the morning, and a dark stuff gown, white apron and cap in the afternoon. The eponymous heroine of George R. Sims's *Mary Jane's Memoirs* (1887) was launched into life from her orphanage with 'a print dress and a stuff dress, and nice new underthings, all marked with my name in red cotton'. Caps were particularly resented as being the badge of servitude. A young servant in *Sketches by Boz* was indignant at 'the tyranny of "Missis"', who wouldn't allow a young girl to wear a short sleeve of an arternoon – no, nor nothing smart, not even a pair of ear-rings; let alone hiding people's heads of hair under them frightful caps'. In 1891 a case was reported of a maid who was discharged after nine days in a new job for refusing to wear a cap. She appealed against unfair dismissal, and the judge ruled that she was not bound to wear one. *Punch* clearly found his verdict ridiculous:

> What shall we do with our Maid?
>   How shall we treat her best?
> Shall the gems that are rare be strewed in her hair?
>   And shall she in silks be drest?
> Shall we make her a gift of gold?
>   Shall we make her our queen? Perhaps.
> But whatever we make her, wherever we take her,
>   We never must make her wear caps.
>
> Imperious, capless, supreme,
>   Do just as you please evermore;
> And wear what you will, for we shall be still,
>   And never complain as before.
> We may put all our money in mines,
>   We may put all our cheese into traps,
> But we put, it is clear, our foot in it, dear,
>   When we try to put you into caps.

8 August 1891

"TOO BAD!"

The New Cook. "WELL, I DECLARE! HERE I'VE BEEN AND GIVE' SIX GUINEAS FOR A NEW DRESS TO KEEP UP THE R'SPECTA-BILITY OF THE 'OUSE, AND HERE'S MISSIS, IN A DOWDY THIRTY SHILLIN' 'ULSTER,' A-COMIN' FROM THAT THERE 'LADIES' CO-OPERATIVE ECONOMICAL MILLINGERY ASSOCIATION'!"

26   *7 February 1880*   27   *19 April 1905*

A MATTER OF HABIT.

Lady (engaging new cook). "ONE THING MORE. I ALWAYS LIKE MY SERVANTS TO DRESS QUIETLY."
Applicant. "OH, THERE WON'T BE ANY TROUBLE ABOUT THAT, MA'AM. I'VE GOT A QUIET TASTE MYSELF."

The average nineteenth-century maid was no longer debarred from following fashion by simple financial considerations, for the booming textile industries had resulted in much cheaper clothes; and her sisters in the factories were taking full advantage of this, without anybody telling them how they should or should not dress. The servant could not help comparing herself with them and finding herself worse off. Flora Thompson describes some of the restrictions in *Lark Rise to Candleford*:

> They had to go to church on Sunday, whether they wanted to or not, and had to leave their best hats with the red roses and ostrich tips in the boxes under their beds and 'make frights of themselves' in funny little flat bonnets. When the Princess of Wales, afterwards Queen Alexandra, set the fashion of wearing the hair in a curled fringe over the forehead, and the fashion spread until it became universal, a fringe was forbidden to maids. They must wear their hair brushed straight back from their brows. A great hardship.

No wonder many maids seem to have had a flamboyant taste in dress on the rare occasions when they could indulge it (Plate 27).

The brothers Mayhew wrote a comical account of a lady's trials in her search for a model maid. One young girl arrives for the job wearing

> . . . *such* a nice plain cotton gown, of only one colour – being a nice white spot on a dark green ground – and *such* a good, strong, serviceable, half-a-crown Dunstable straw bonnet, trimmed very plainly; and *such* a nice clean quilled net-cap under it; and *such* a tidy plain white muslin collar over one of the quietest black-and-white plaid shawls I think I ever saw in all my life, that I felt quite charmed at seeing her dressed *so* thoroughly like what a respectable servant ought to be.

But the very next Sunday, things have changed:

> . . . for lo and behold! my neat, unpretending chrysalis had changed into a flaunting fal-lal butterfly. . . . Bless us and save us! if the stuck-up thing hadn't got on a fly-a-way starched-out Balzorina gown, of a bright ultramarine, picked out with white flowers – with a double skirt, too, made like a tunic, and looking *so* grand (though one could easily see that it could not possibly have cost more than six-and-six – if that, indeed), and drat her

impudence! if she hadn't on each side of her head got a bunch of long ringlets, like untwisted bell-ropes, hanging half down to her waist, and a blonde-lace cap, with cherry-coloured rosettes, and streamers flying about nearly a yard long; while on looking at her feet, if the conceited bit of goods hadn't got on patent leather shoes, with broad sandals, and open-worked cotton stockings, as I'm a living woman – and net mittens on her hands too, as true as my name's Sk-n-st-n.

In the Mayhews' story the antagonism between mistress and maid is aggravated by the fact that Susan is younger and prettier than her employer. This was doubtless a common enough situation (Plate 28).

The crinoline typifies the Victorians' attitude to their servants' dress. It was the first fashion to be universally adopted by all ages and

28　*II, 1847, p. 200*

DOMESTIC BLISS.

Domestic (soliloquising). " WELL ! I'M SURE MISSUS HAD BETTER GIVE THIS NEW BONNET TO ME, INSTEAD OF STICKING SUCH A YOUNG-LOOKING THING UPON HER OLD SHOULDERS." (*The impudent minx has immediate warning.*)

SERVANTGALISM.

Mary. "Did you call, Mum?"

Lady. "Yes, Mary! I thought I told you not to wear your Hoop before you had done your Rooms, because you broke the Jugs and Basins with it!"

Mary. "Oh, Mum! You see the *Sweeps* were coming this Morning, and, really, I could not think of opening the Door to them such a Figger as I should ha' been without my Crinoline!"

29 *21 November 1863*

classes, for it could be cheaply produced, and it provided the wearer with such a distinctive appearance that not to wear it was to look strange (Plate 29). Furthermore, it could be worn underneath any kind of dress, whether a ball gown or a maid's uniform. It was undeniably extremely impractical, so that the complaints of mistresses that it was inappropriate for housework would seem well founded. China did get knocked over (Plate 30). Worse, cooks were burned to death when their distended skirts caught in the fire. And yet, when crinolines had gone out of fashion and ladies had adopted a newer craze, the servants were positively expected to continue wearing them. As *Punch* expressed it:

> No more ladies death will find,
> In their frames of steel calcined,
> Set on blazes by a grate without a screen;
> Though some cookmaids yet may flare,
> Who dress out, and don't take care,
> For the servants still will wear,
> > Crinoline.

25 March 1865

And the maid who too hastily jettisons hers to be in the mode is met not with approval but with her notice (Plate 31).

At the beginning of the Victorian period it was considered quite ludicrous that servants should care about their appearance beyond the calls of mere cleanliness (Plates 32 and 33), and the suggestion that a maid might read a fashion magazine was sufficient to provoke hilarity (Plate 34). *Punch* offered the following facetious advice to would-be nursery maids:

> It is not necessary to give you any particular directions about your dress, for the penny *Belle Assemblee* will furnish you with all the latest fashions; and you have only to do in cottons and stuffs, what your mistress is doing in silks and satins. You should bear in mind, that you are not obliged to make yourself a dowdy to please any one; for nature has doubtless given you a pretty face, and the gifts of nature ought to be made the most of. Besides, if you are a servant at home, you are a lady out of doors; and you may even keep a parasol at the greengrocer's, to be ready for you when you take a holiday.
>
> II, 1845, p. 19

CAUSE AND EFFECT.

Housemaid. "Drat the bothering China cups and things. They be always a-knocking up against one's Crinoline."

30   *26 March 1864*

"LIKE HER IMPUDENCE."

Missis and the Young Ladies (together). "GOODNESS GRACIOUS, J'MIMA! WHAT HAVE YOU——*WHERE'S* YOUR CR'N'LIN?" (*This word snappishly.*)

Jemima. "OH 'M, PLEASE 'M, WHICH I UNDERSTOOD AS THEY WAS A GOIN' OUT, 'M——"   [*Receives warning on the spot.*

31   *4 July 1866*

32   *18 August 1855*   33   *12 August 1876*

" *You'm no call to laugh, young man. My complexion's as much a objeck to me as the first Lady of the Land's is hern.*"

EQUALITY.

Maid (before the Party). "SHALL YOU WEAR YOUR WHITE MUSLIN TO-NIGHT, MA'AM?"
Mistress. "YES, JANE!"
Maid. "THEN I'LL WEAR MY BLUE SILK, AS I DON'T WANT US TO CLASH!"

Enter MARY *the Housemaid with the Morning Letters.*

OLD LADY (who has seen the 'delivery' through the blinds). "*But there was a book or a paper, Mary, I thought I saw——*"

MARY. "*Only this 'ere Mum, which it's for me, Mum, the ''Lustrated Penny Weekly Bell Assembly,' Mum, as I takes in myself reg'lar.*"

Very gradually, however, as the century progressed, mistresses had to get used to the idea that their servants wished to keep up with fashion; and when it was announced, at the end of 1875, that a society was to be set up, and that 'the prevailing love of finery evinced by female domestic servants is to be taken in hand, and awards in money are to be offered as encouragement to servant-girls to dress more suitably to their stations in life', it was clearly something of a last-ditch stand. *Punch*'s own sympathies came down firmly on the side of the servants, and were expressed in 'Mary Anner on Modes and Missises':

Dear Susan Jane, You've heard, no doubt, of this Association
For making people dress theirselves according to their station;
Which what they sez they're aiming at is putting of a stopper
On fashions as is 'stravagant, or hurtful or improper . . .
Encourage Servant-Girls to dress as suits their situation?
O yes, I dessay! Very fine! I've heard *that* observation
A goodish many times before, from lips of lots of Missises
As though nice toggery weren't for all, the same as food and kisses is!
Which service ain't no 'eritage at best, but plague upon it
If a girl can't have a sweetheart, or a Sunday-best smart bonnet . . .
To put us into uniform's their game; dear Sue, don't heed 'em,
But let us Servants all unite, and stick up for our freedom.

SIC TRANSIT !

35   *28 August 1880*   ALAS, FOR THE PRETTY JERSEY COSTUME ! 'ANDSOME 'ARRIET, THE 'OUSEMAID, HAS GOT IT AT LAST, AND IT FITS HER JUST AS WELL AS HER MISSUS.

If Missises hates 'finery', they've only got to drop it,
But bribing Servant-girls they'll find is not the way to stop it.
If they'd have us laugh at fashion, let 'em set us the example,
Before they frowns at our fal-lals, and on our feelin's trample.
No! 'Sunday Best for Ever!' is the motto for our banner,
Down with Mob-caps and Missises!

Yours truly,

MARY ANNER.

1 January 1876

There was still a feeling, which persisted long into our own century, that a fashion was devalued if it was adopted by the working class (Plates 35 and 36), but now the time-lag became shorter and shorter (Plate 37). Ladies still attempted to control their servants' dress, but by the last third of the century there was considerably more latitude than had existed in the 1840s (Plates 38 and 39). This was partly because the increased opportunities for employment outside the domestic sphere had led to a shortage of servants, and those who were left could afford to be slightly more self-assertive. Better and more widespread schooling, and more and more women earning their living in clerical and educational jobs, led to greater flexibility in the old social structures, so that it became harder to tell a person's station by her clothes. Thus, on

ANOTHER BLOW FOR OXFORD.

36   *22 April 1925*

37   *9 May 1906*

Mistress (soliloquizing). "I'M AFRAID THIS HAT 'S RATHER OUT OF DATE."
Maid. "OH NO, MUM. IT'S QUITE FASHIONABLE. COOK HAS JUST BOUGHT ONE EXACTLY LIKE IT!"

HEIGHT OF LUXURY.

"Lor! Mary Anne! Do your Missis let you 'ave a 'Dolly Varding!'"

38   *24 August 1872*

39   *10 August 1895*

THE BICYCLE AGAIN.

Applicant for the Situation of Cook. "Before I go, please, Ma'am, may I ask your Servant to show me the Basement? I must see that you have a convenient place for my Bicycle!"

Mistress. "Of course I have seen to that. You will find a Room set apart. Only I must tell you that I don't allow Rational Dress!"

the eve of the Great War, we find the lady and her gardener's daughter dressed identically (Plate 40).

During the war large numbers of servants left the home and took up the jobs left vacant by their absent menfolk. Some of them commanded much larger salaries than before – it was a matter of scandal that the girls in the munitions factories could afford fur coats, and clearly the men there were natty dressers too (Plate 41) – many of them revelling in their new freedom from domestic restrictions. When the war was over a large number of them stayed on in their new sphere and the shortage of servants became acute. It is unlikely that any of them dictated their terms or commanded the huge wages which the jokes would have us believe (Plates 42 and 43), but the fact that the jokes exist suggests that the balance of power had shifted a little.

Another factor which encouraged the levelling out of dress distinctions was the rise of ready-to-wear. The economic stringencies and the practical necessities of the war had resulted in a radical simplification of women's dress, and it was at last possible to buy a perfectly acceptable

40   *24 April 1912*

OUR SNOBS.

Her Ladyship. "Isn't that my gardener's daughter, Giles?"
Giles. "Yes, yer ladyship; quite a mistake, touching my 'at to 'er. Why, she's as poor as I be."

Mistress (to maid who has asked for a rise). "WHY, MARY, I CANNOT POSSIBLY GIVE YOU AS MUCH AS THAT."

Mary. "WELL, MA'AM, YOU SEE, THE GENTLEMAN I WALK OUT WITH HAS JUST GOT A JOB IN A MUNITION FACTORY, AND I SHALL BE OBLIGED TO DRESS UP TO HIM."

Lady (to prospective daily housemaid). "THE HOURS WILL BE FROM NINE TO SIX-THIRTY, WITH AN HOUR AND A-HALF OFF FOR DINNER."

D. H. "FOR LUNCHEON, I SUPPOSE YOU MEAN. AND I SHOULD HAVE TO LEAVE AT SIX, AS I ALWAYS DINE AT MY CLUB AND HAVE TO DRESS FIRST."

"THAT'S BETTY GRANT'S NEW MAID."   "SHE'S MUCH SMARTER THAN HER MISTRESS."

"WELL, THEY CAN'T *BOTH* AFFORD TO DRESS LIKE THAT."

43   *16 March 1921*   44   *22 October 1919*

Lady (who has purchased a ready-made dress at the local draper's). "TIRESOME THIS DRESS IS. THE FASTENERS COME UNDONE AS QUICK AS YOU DO THEM UP."

Cook (acting lady's-maid). "YES, 'M, THEY DO. THAT'S WHY I WOULDN'T HAVE IT MYSELF WHEN I TRIED IT ON AT THE SHOP THE OTHER DAY."

outfit off the peg. No longer could social distinctions be expressed in the
quantity of trimming on a dress: while there were still, of course, cheap
clothes and expensive clothes, it was possible for a lady and her cook to
contemplate buying the same dress (Plate 44). And once that point had
been reached and accepted, there was no longer any point in making
jokes about what the servants wore.

2   The Venus of Milo

Dresses, unlike other objects of decorative art, have only a limited identity of their own. A Wedgwood teacup remains the same, no matter who is drinking out of it – even sitting in a glass case it is still the same. But a dress on a hanger is incomplete. It needs a body to fill it, and even then it is changeable because it will take on the identity of the wearer and be ugly or beautiful, tasteful or vulgar, depending on her. But the power of fashion is such that, while the dress assumes the shape of the wearer, the wearer has already moulded that shape in response to the dress, or at least in response to the prevailing fashion. A glance through any illustrated costume history shows that at different times people, and especially women, have achieved radically different outlines while always starting from the same basic material. Now they will have large monolithic bosoms, now flat chests; now they will be Junoesque, now look like half-starved waifs; now their bottoms will jut out, now they will disappear completely and all the emphasis will be on the shoulders. Of course a certain amount can be achieved by padding, but the two chief ways of moulding the body into a given shape are corsetry and dieting.

In the Victorian age dieting was virtually unknown. The aim of the modern girl, to be as thin as possible all over, would in any case have been incomprehensible to her great-grandmother. The ideal Victorian girl had nicely covered arms and shoulders, plump but not fat, and a shapely bust. Her hips and legs had no importance because, under all her petticoats, they were neither seen nor even hinted at, but her waist was as tiny as she could make it. This sort of figure could not have been achieved by dieting anyway: it demanded, quite simply, a good corset.

Corsets were made of a stout material like jean or cotton satin, stiffened with strips of whalebone or steel, and they fastened up the back with laces threaded through eyelet holes. At the beginning of our period they were long, supported by shoulder straps, gusseted at the bust and hips and with a channel down the middle of the front, into which was

CASE X.—A LADY OF FASHION.

This is the wife of a nobleman, in full dress. It will be seen that the barbarian English have no notion whatever of " the golden lilies " *

* The " golden lilies " are, poetically, the little distorted feet of the Chinese women.

45   *I, 1844, p. 221*

slotted a busk, a rigid, slightly curved piece of wood or whalebone which ensured an erect carriage. As skirts grew fuller and fuller, however, and developed into the crinoline, corsets became shorter, shoulder straps disappeared and the busk was replaced with steel fastenings. The back laces remained, as these were the means of tightening the corset until the waist had reached the required measurement. Corsets, or stays, were considered so essential to a good figure that quite small girls were put into them, and were often not allowed to remove them even at night. The obvious parallel with the Chinese custom of foot-binding was pointed out by *Punch*. In 1844 an exhibition was held in London of Chinese ways and customs: *Punch* published a spoof catalogue of an 'Exhibition of the English in China', and used it to satirize English society (Plate 45).

CASE X. - A LADY OF FASHION

This is the wife of a nobleman, in full dress. . . . The poor women of England are, almost from their cradles, made the victims of a horrible custom. It is supposed that thousands and thousands die yearly from a disease called Tite Lace In. The female child is taken at a very early age, and has its stomach compressed by a machine called Sta Iz, which is ribbed with steel and whale-bone . . . and is corded tightly up the back. This Sta Iz is never, up to the time of womanhood, taken off; as is plain from the specimen here presented. The barbarians have a laughable notion of the use of this custom: they think that, by making the waist no thicker than the arm, it gives beauty to the female – a melancholy bigotry. . . .

I, 1844, p. 222

Although the death-toll has obviously been exaggerated in this description, women did undoubtedly suffer illness and even death from tight-lacing. Since they could not breathe properly they were subject to giddiness and fainting, and in time their internal organs could become severely crushed and displaced, which accounts partly for the notoriously difficult time many women had in childbirth. A couple of years later *Punch* returned to the attack, pointing out that many unpleasant results could be expected from tight-lacing, among them red noses, swollen hands and feet, curvature of the spine and headaches. 'This perhaps alone would be a trifle; but lacing involves short life: and as the contracted figure suggests a resemblance to the hour-glass, the hour-glass suggests a warning to the contracted figure' (I, 1846, p. 238).

One of the few aspects of the bloomer costume to gain *Punch*'s approval was its opposition to tight-lacing: it had after all been modelled on the dress worn by ladies in Swiss sanatoriums who were recovering from the effects of excessive corseting. But the bloomer costume lasted only six months, and tight-lacing showed no signs of abating, despite threats and coaxing:

> So you think, young ladies, do you, that men like a slim waist? Well, so they may perhaps, if it be one of Nature's moulding. But when Nature makes a slender waist, she makes it lithe and lissome, and that is what your staymakers by no art can accomplish. When a man has the good fortune to get hold of a girl's waist, he likes to feel it soft and yielding, and not buckramed and bone-stiffened. . . . So, ladies, dear kind silly thoughtless loving lovely ladies, do let common sense for once gain admittance to the fashion-books. . . . We know you dress to please us (at least you tell your husbands so), and depend on it, dear ladies, there is not a man among us – not being a born fool – that does not hate, detest, abominate, and occasionally swear at the sinful, suicidal fashion of tight-lacing, which is every whit as frightful a personal disfigurement as the squeezed skulls of the Flat-Heads, or the crushed feet of the Chinese.
>
> 19 September 1863

Interest in the subject grew, and by the late 1860s the *English-woman's Domestic Magazine* was receiving such a volume of correspondence about it that it published a special supplement to cope with it. The letters throw much light on this strange topic, and reveal so clearly its psychosexual aspect – one young girl referring to the 'delicious sensations, half pleasure half pain' induced by tight-lacing – that they are now classified as pornography in the British Library. One example will suffice to show how far some women were prepared to go in pursuit of a small waist:

> I did not commence to lace tightly until I was married, nor should I have done so then had not my husband been so particularly fond of a small waist; but I was determined not to lose one atom of his affection for the sake of a little trouble. I could not bear to think of him liking any one else's figure better than mine, consequently, although my waist measured twenty-three inches, I went and ordered a pair of stays, made very strong and filled with stiff bone, measuring only fourteen inches round the waist. These, with the assistance of my maid, I put on, and managed the first day to lace my waist in eighteen inches. At night I slept in the corset without loosing the lace in the least. The next day my maid got my waist to seventeen inches, and so on an inch smaller every day until she got them to meet.
>
> I wore them regularly without ever taking them off, having them tightened afresh every day, as the lace might stretch a little.
>
> They did not open in front, so that I could not undo them if I had wanted. For the first day the pain was very great, but as soon as the stays were laced close, and I had worn them so for a few days, I began to care nothing about it, and in a month or so I would not have taken them off on any account, for I quite enjoyed the sensation, and when I let my husband see me with a dress to fit I was amply repaid for my trouble; and although I am now grown older, and the fresh bloom of youth is gone from my cheek, still my figure remains the same, which is a charm age will not rob me of. I have never had cause to regret the step I took.
>
> quoted in *Punch*, 8 February 1868

Punch declared that this letter was not genuine, but 'the irony of a wise and clever man'. Certainly the specimens surviving in museums today suggest that the 14-inch waist was a myth: even 19-inch waists are rare; the most usual are between 21 and 23 inches – small, certainly, but not to the point of deformity. Whatever the end-product, however, tight-lacing itself was a reality, and so were its effects. In 1869 the *Morning Post* reported the case of a nineteen-year-old nursery maid who collapsed dead while out walking a child in a pram. 'It was discovered that she was very tightly laced, and DR SMELLIE stated that death was caused by effusion of blood on the brain, caused by fatty heart, accelerated by compression of the chest produced by tight-lacing.' Outraged once more, *Punch* declared that

> . . . the typical and average woman can no more deviate from the dress of the day than an animal can choose to change its skin or its spots. There is no fear that any girls accustomed to tight-lacing will ever be induced to relinquish that practice which renders them such delightful objects to one another, if ridiculous and repulsive to stupid men, by any such nonsense as a report of the verdict of a coroner's jury ascribing death to the effect of tight-lacing in accelerating fatty degeneration of the heart.

2 October 1869

By 1870 tight-lacing was as drastic as ever, but a totally new outline had been given to the figure by the increasing popularity of high-heeled shoes and boots. These had been around for a decade or more, but by

"THE GRECIAN BEND."

Does not Tight-Lacing and High Heels give a Charming Grace and Dignity to the Female Figure?

46   *2 October 1869*

THE VENUS OF MILO; OR, GIRLS OF TWO DIFFERENT PERIODS.

Chorus. "Look at her Big Foot! Oh, What a Waist!—and what a Ridiculous Little Head!—and no Chignon! She's no Lady! Oh, what a Fright!"

THAT CLASSICAL CURVE AGAIN!

Agnes (just engaged). "Papa, dear, I am going for a Walk, to meet Charles."
Papa (who will have his joke). "All right, Agnes. But now, you've got a Beau, wouldn't it Match better if you Looked a little more like an Arrow?"

FASHIONABLE EMULATION.

Lady (speaking with difficulty). "WHAT HAVE YOU MADE IT ROUND THE WAIST, MRS. PRICE?"
Dressmaker. "TWENTY-ONE INCHES, MA'AM. YOU COULDN'T *BREATHE* WITH LESS!"
Lady. "WHAT'S LADY JEMIMA JONES'S WAIST?"
Dressmaker. "NINETEEN-AND-A-HALF JUST NOW, MA'AM. BUT HER LADYSHIP'S A HEAD SHORTER THAN YOU ARE, AND SHE'S GOT EVER SO MUCH THINNER SINCE HER ILLNESS LAST AUTUMN!"
Lady. "THEN MAKE IT *NINETEEN*, MRS. PRICE, AND *I'LL* ENGAGE TO GET INTO IT!"

49 *28 July 1877*

now they had adopted the characteristic 'Louis' shape, slim and waisted, and had risen as high as 2 inches. Medical authorities condemned them roundly:

> The absurd and ungainly practice of mounting the hinder part of the feet on stilts whilst the toes press the ground and bear the weight, is one against which it is not easy to write with temper. The device of strangling the waist with tightly-laced corsets was contemptible for its ignorance; that to which we now allude is outrageous in its defiance of the laws of gravity. . . .
>
> *The Lancet*, 1878

Together with the heavy masses of hair, often false, which were piled on to the back of the head, the tiny waist and high heels tilted the whole body forwards into the characteristic, and much derided, 'Grecian Bend' (Plates 46, 47 and 48). In vain did writers of girls' books like Sarah Tytler describe a heroine who abjured high heels and 'would well nigh have mounted a scaffold where she might have died nobly for the sake of God and her conscience, and the love of her friends and neighbours, sooner than perish most ignobly by pinching her waist till

HYGIENIC EXCESS.

THE O'FARRELL-MACKENZIE GIRLS HAVE GONE IN SO EXTENSIVELY FOR EARLY RISING, FRESH AIR, COLD WATER, FARINACEOUS FOOD, ROWING, RIDING, RINKING, LAWN-TENNIS, GYMNASTICS, AND WHAT NOT, THAT THEY HAVE DISTORTED THEIR FIGURES INTO THE LIKENESS OF SO MANY GREEK STATUES, AND HAVE NO MORE WAIST TO SPEAK OF THAN THAT QUITE TOO HORRID VENUS AT THE LOUVRE; INDEED THEY HAVE GIVEN UP STAYS ALTOGETHER AS A BAD JOB. AS THEY ARE ALL ENGAGED TO MARRY DUKES, MR. PUNCH FEARS THEY WILL SET THE FASHION; AND AS HE HOLDS THAT A LONG AND WASP-LIKE WAIST IS AS ESSENTIAL TO A LADY AS A— WELL, AS A HUMP BETWEEN THE SHOULDERS, A PROMINENT NOSE AND CHIN, AND A PROTUBERANT ABDOMEN ARE TO A GENTLEMAN, HE HOPES THAT THE ABOVE CARICATURE MAY SERVE AS AN EXAMPLE AND A WARNING.

50   *18 October 1879*

her body resembled an hourglass'; most girls were glad to suffer if they could thereby gain a smaller waist than their rivals' (Plate 49). To what extent public opinion encouraged them is hard to say. *Punch* never tired of reiterating that men found tight-laced waists repulsive; yet when it published its picture of the O'Farrell-Mackenzie girls, athletic Amazons with generous, uncorseted waists, it is pretty clear that they were not held up for serious admiration (Plate 50).

Not only did fashion dictate the shape of waists: bosoms, too, rose and fell according to her decree.

When a lady of Mr Punch's acquaintance was in Paris not very long ago, she ordered a dress at a famous *Modiste*'s, but found, when she tried it on, that she could hardly breathe. On her complaining to the *Modiste* that the dress was too tight over the chest,

'Que voulez-vous, Madame?' exclaimed that faithful follower – if not framer – of the fashion. 'On ne porte plus de gorge.' ('Bosoms are not worn now.')

'Qu'est-ce-qu'on fait donc?' ('But how do ladies manage?') asked her innocent English customer.

SHOPPING !

Lady (at Sea-side "Emporium"). "How much are those—ah—Improvers!"
Shopman. "Improv—hem!—They 're not, Ma'am"—(confused)—"not—not the article you require, Ma'am. They 're Fencing-Masks, Ma'am!" [Tableau!]

51   *25 December 1886*

A MODERN WAIST.

Jones (to himself, as he offers Miss Vane a cup of tea and some straw-berries). "By Jove! she takes 'em—she 's going to Swallow 'em! But where she 'll put 'em—goodness knows!"

52   *10 August 1889*

'Mais, dame, on ote la ouate' ('Oh! they take out the wadding'), was the equally innocent answer.

Punch had never fully appreciated the bearings of this perfectly true story till the other day when he came upon the following paragraph in one of the leading ladies' journals:–

'Buy a pair of Maintenon corsets, fitting your waist measure. The other parts of the corset will be proportioned as you ought to be. Put the corset on, and fill the vacant space with fine jeweller's wool, then tack on a piece of soft silk or cambric over the bust thus formed to keep the wool in place, renewing it as often as required. This is the most natural and effectual mode of improving the figure which I have heard of.'

24 February 1877

As the crinoline subsided and skirt drapery was drawn increasingly to the back of the dress, in the late 1860s and early 1870s, the front was more exposed. Until this time the substructure of the skirt had followed a fairly simple line, achieved first by a number of petticoats, with a small crescent-shaped pad supporting the extra fullness at the back, and then by the wire crinoline. The outline was hemispherical, and bore no relation to the body underneath, which was free to take any shape it liked. In the 1870s, however, the bustle which shaped the back of the skirt became more complex, consisting either of half-hoops built into a fabric petticoat, or of a series of stiff horsehair frills, while at the front the fabric of the dress was stretched so tightly that the stomach required flattening. Corsets lengthened again, and by the next decade the rigid panel down the middle of the front curved and widened at the bottom into the 'spoon' shape, which effectively controlled bulging tummies. During the 1880s the bustle reappeared, but this time it was an angular, totally artificial shape that jutted out at right angles to the back and was achieved either by a long, concertina-shaped half-petticoat or by a stiff hemispherical contraption known as an 'improver' (Plate 51).

In the 1890s elaborate skirt drapery was abandoned, and the skirt, now gored, fitted smoothly over the hips. Tiny waists were more *de rigueur* than ever, emphasized by huge sleeves and wide belts (Plate 52), and the close fit of the skirt meant that the long corset was still a necessity. Gwen Raverat remembered the clothes of the time:

> The thought of the discomfort, restraint and pain, which we had to endure from our clothes, makes me even angrier now than it did then; for in those days nearly everyone accepted their inconveniences as inevitable. Except for the most small-waisted, naturally dumb-bell-shaped females, the ladies never seemed at ease, or even quite as if they were wearing their own clothes. For their dresses were always made too tight, and the bodices wrinkled laterally from the strain; and their stays showed in a sharp ledge across the middles of their backs. And in spite of whalebone, they were apt to bulge below the waist in front; for, poor dears, they were but human after all, and they had to expand somewhere. . . . Whenever I went to stay with Aunt Etty, soon after my arrival, I would feel her fingers fumbling in my waist-belt, to make sure that I was not tight-lacing; for she suspected every young person of a wish to be fashionable. She used to tell us a dreadful moral tale about a lady who laced herself so hard that she cut her liver *right in half*, and died in consequence.

Girls were still fitted with corsets before they were fully grown, for she goes on:

Margaret says that the first time she was put into them – when she wa about thirteen – she ran round and round the nursery screaming with rage. I did not do that. I simply went away and took them off; endured sullenly the row which ensued, when my soft-shelled condition was discovered; was forcibly re-corseted; and, as soon as possible went away and took them off again. One of my governesses used to weep over my wickedness in this respect. I had a bad figure, and to me they were real instruments of torture; they prevented me from breathing, and dug deep holes into my softer parts on every side. I am sure no hair-shirt could have been worse to me.

The clear, crisp lines of the 1890s gave way to the more flowing curves of the Edwardian style. Skirts were cleverly cut and gored to produce a soft bell shape, sleeves were full to the wrist and then gathered into tight cuffs which they overhung, and bodices were pouched to give the look of a pouter pigeon. Bosoms were monolithic, and the body assumed an S-shape reminiscent of the Grecian bend, but very much more feminine, thanks to the fluid lines of the skirt. Waists were still small, but were no longer the focal point of the dress, and the worst days of tight-lacing were over. When a fashion column announced that 'the latest mode demands that the waist must measure its natural circumference, and must be twenty-four inches, at least', *Punch* hailed this as 'Woman's Franchise':

> At Fashion's edict, stern and brief –
>   'The waist must be compressed no more' –
> A suspiration of relief
>   Goes up from shore to shore.
>
> Behold the triumph of the plump!
>   Her ample symmetry she hastes
> To blazon boldly, while a slump
>   Occurs in willow waists.
>
> For 'twenty-four' is *chic*, no less;
>   And maids too slender by an inch
> To save themselves from dowdiness
>   Will have to pad, not pinch.
>
> While multitudes of cords and bands
>   And tapes, uncomfortably tense,
> Spring looser now the mode demands
>   A wide circumference.

Man gives the fashion his support
   With approbation deep and strong,
For tempers will not be so short
   Nor doctor's bills so long.

In fact, the female form divine
   Once more will transiently reign,
Now Paris follows Nature's line
   And ladies breathe again.

7 April 1909

THE

SPAT-
CORSET

ONLY
30 G^{ns}

SPECIALLY DESIGNED TO MEET THE EVER-
GROWING TASTE FOR LONGER AND LONGER
CORSETS.

53   *24 January 1912*

"DRESS AND UNDRESS."

First Guest. "THAT MRS. ASTERISK'S A PRETTY WOMAN, AND SHE AIN'T BADLY GOT UP; BUT SHE LOOKS ALL WRONG SOMEHOW."
Second Guest. "OF COURSE SHE DOES. THE RIDICULOUS WOMAN PERSISTS IN WEARING HER BACKBONE, AND BACKBONES ARE QUITE GONE OUT."

54   *23 July 1913*

In the decade preceding the Great War, fashion, partly owing to the influence of Paul Poiret, adopted a vertical look strongly reminiscent of the neoclassical styles of a century earlier. Skirts were straight and slim, frills and froth were eliminated, and the corset reached its longest yet (Plate 53). The correct posture to accompany this look was not straight and erect, but limp and droopy, calling to mind the paintings of David (Plate 54). *Punch* described the look thus:

> Long languid lines unbroken by a frill,
> Superfluous festoons reduced to *nil*,
> A figure like a seal reared up on end
> And poking forward with a studied bend;
>
> A shortish neck imprisoned in a ruff,
> Skin-fitting sleeves that show a stint of stuff,
> A waist promoted halfway up the back,
> And not a shred that's comfortably slack;
>
> A multitude of buttons, row on row,
> Not there for business – merely meant for show,
> A skirt whose meagre gores necessitate
> The waddle of a Chinese lady's gait;

A 'busby' toque extinguishing the hair
As if a giant hand had crushed it there –
Behold the latest mode! and write beneath,
'A winter blossom bursting from its "sheath".'

30 December 1908

The Great War could not fail to influence fashion profoundly, and while economy and practicality decreed the retention of the linear look, sloppy posture now appeared to denote unpatriotic apathy. 'Deportment for Women' outlined the new ideal:

SISTERS, when fashion first decreed
To our devoted sex
That beauty must be broken-kneed
And spinal cords convex;
When sheathlike skirts without a crease
Were potent to attract,
Those were the piping times of peace,
When everybody slacked.

But, since the menace of 'The Day'
Has commandeered the Nut,
Since *demi-saison* modes display
A military cut,
It's up to us to do our bit
Each time we take the road,
For, if we wear a warlike kit,
The mien must match the *mode*.

What! would you set a 'forage cap'
Upon a drooping brow?
The feet that used to mince and tap
Must stride with vigour now;
No longer must a plastic crouch
Debilitate the knees;
We've finished with the 'Slinker Slouch';
Heads up, girls, if you please!

20 January 1915

At the end of the war the vertical look was still going strong, but it had now become positively tubular. Corsets as such were a thing of the

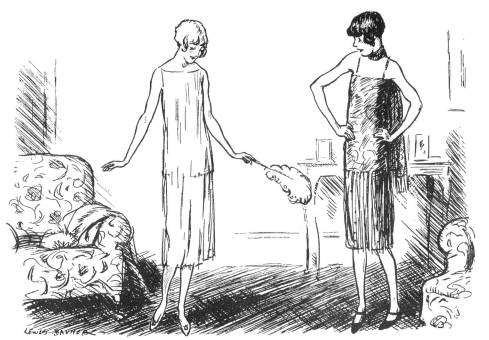

Second-Season Young Lady (to débutante). "YES, THE FROCK'S NOT BAD, AND YOUR HEAD'S ALL RIGHT; BUT, MY DEAR CHILD, YOU HOLD YOURSELF SHOCKINGLY. WHY, YOU'RE POSITIVELY GRACEFUL!"

55   *26 November 1924*

56   *6 February 1924*

MANNERS AND MODES.

Angry Young Lady. "I HATE HER! SHE SAYS SUCH CATTY THINGS. SHE JUST TOLD ME I HAD A PRETTY FIGURE."
Her Companion. "BUT—PARDON ME—WHY IS THAT SO OFFENSIVE?"
Angry Young Lady. "OH, SURELY EVEN YOU MUST KNOW THAT FIGURES ARE HOPELESSLY OUT OF FASHION!"

past, breasts were flattened by bandeaux, waists were abolished by the totally unshaped dresses which strove to equalize women's vital statistics, and the fashionable posture was now, at worst, a studied gracelessness (Plates 55 and 56), and at best a hard jauntiness borrowed from the world of sport. Jordan Baker, the golf-playing confidant in Scott Fitzgerald's *Great Gatsby*, 'was a slender, small-breasted girl, with an erect carriage, which she accentuated by throwing her body backward at the shoulders like a young cadet'. Later the narrator observes that 'she wore her evening-dress, all her dresses, like sports clothes – there was a jauntiness about her movements as if she had first learned to walk upon golf courses on clean, crisp mornings'. And Iris Storm, the fast-living heroine and wearer of Michael Arlen's *Green Hat*, 'stood carelessly, like the women in Georges Barbier's almanacks . . . who know how to stand carelessly. Her hands were thrust into the pockets of a light brown leather jacket – *pour le sport* – which shone quite definitely in the lamplight: it was wide open at the throat, and had a high collar of

57   *21 December 1927*

MANNERS AND MODES.

Old Lady (at her first mannequin parade, very audibly). "MY DEAR, I'M POSITIVE THAT AN INQUIRY IS NEEDED INTO THE WORKING CONDITIONS OF THESE GIRLS. THE POOR THINGS LOOK HALF-STARVED."

he fur of a few minks'.

To complete this boyish and athletic image, the figure was
equired to be extremely slim, to the bewilderment of the older
eneration, who remembered when women had been women (Plate
•7). Thus it is during the 1920s that we find the first mention of weight-
onsciousness, which has haunted us ever since. For perhaps the first
ime in history the woman who wanted to fit into a smaller dress did
aot resort to corsetry. This was partly because the very much simpler
and skimpier dresses would have been inadequate to conceal a full-
ledged Victorian-style corset; it was also because women were no
onger prepared to impair their own freedom of movement. The 1920s,
and more especially the 1930s, saw a craze for health manifested in
utdoor exercise, in a new interest in diet, and in a much greater
xposure of the body linked with a cult of the suntan. Methods of
veight reduction accorded with these new ideas and consisted either of
tarvation (Plates 58 and 59), or of special exercises, often with the help

RESOLUTION.

Husband. "JOAN'S JUST RUNG UP—WANTS US TO DINE THERE ON THURSDAY."
Wife. "TELL HER I'M NOT EATING ANYTHING THIS YEAR."

58   *7 January 1931*

of patent machines (Plate 60). It was essential that the whole body
should be in good shape, since it was now all on view. The rigour
undergone in pursuit of slimness caused *Punch* to look back with
nostalgia to the supposed golden age when ladies were simply measured
and fitted for their dresses regardless of shape (Plate 61). As we have
seen, this idea was totally illusory.

Although the fashions of the 1930s still required women to be
extremely slim, there was a change from the previous decade. The
overall shape was very much more feminine, with the waist defined at its
natural level, and signs of a bust; and skirts lengthened again. The new
look required a radical change in posture, from the jaunty to the
sinuous, which some people clearly found difficult to acquire (Plate 62)
just as, in 1969, the leggy miniskirt stride with knees to the fore looked
clumsy and inappropriate when shrouded in a maxi. But the change was
made, and woman's ability to alter her shape at fashion's whim
prompted *Punch*'s 'Willow Song':

59   *11 January 1933*

THE SLIMMING CRAZE.

Doctor. "AND DO YOU DRINK AT MEALS?"
Patient. "DON'T BE SILLY, DOCTOR. WHY, I DON'T EVEN *EAT* AT MEALS."

When Fashion said to the girl, 'Be slim',
  And each, in her wondrous way,
Grew slight of body and light of limb,
  And all in a single day;
When never a flounce or frill was seen,
And never a curve where curves had been,
And the feminine leg (an engrossing member)
  Gave us a long display –

I gave my heart to the willowy girl;
  I said, 'She is more my line
Than the fluffed-out puffed-out billowy girl
  That yesterday called divine;
I like her slender, I like her light;
The whole effect is exactly right;
And I'll take my oath that the pillowy girl
  Shall never be love of mine.'

60 *9 January 1929*

Mother. " DARLINGS, WHAT *ARE* YOU DOING ? "
Peter. " PEGGY'S GOT SO FAT SINCE CHRISTMAS, AND WE'RE REDUCING HER. "

And now, when Fashion again has swerved,
  And every girl of taste
Must be well-covered and neatly-curved,
  With signs, I'm told, of a waist;
When frills and flounces are all the go,
And a mild demeanour is comme il faut,
And legs, they say, will be tamely hidden
  By petticoats long and laced –

I give my heart to the billowy girl,
  As a flowery thing to see,
For the dancing prancing willowy girl
  Is not what a girl should be;
If Eve had a figure (as I believe)
Then all Eve's daughters should be like Eve,
And I feel convinced that the pillowy girl
  Is really the girl for me.

                                    12 September 1928

Precisely as the 1913 droop straightened up for the First World
War, so the curvaceous and feminine 1930s look gave way to an erect
stance and firm posture at the beginning of the Second World War, the
aura of dauntless courage being enhanced by shoulder padding. At the
end of the war, to the disgust of economists and feminists alike, Christian
Dior launched his controversial and highly nostalgic 'New Look', which
not only brought skirts back down almost to the ankles, but
reintroduced figures reminiscent of Victorian times, and achieved by
quasi-Victorian means. Brigid Keenan describes them:

Dior's dresses may have looked more curvy and natural than the
austere wartime ones, but what went on underneath to produce
that effect became a legend in itself. A Dior dress had so much
scaffolding inside that it could almost stand up alone. The fabric of
each one was lined with tulle and that in turn was lined with fine
silk to prevent it scratching or laddering stockings. There was
padding and pleating to shape all the skirts out over hips, and
bodices over busts. There were special boned corsets made of black
tulle for each dress to cinch in the waist and push up the breasts:
sometimes these were frilled on hip and bra cup to achieve an even
more curvy shape. Evening dresses had the corsets built in so that
the wearer had only to step in, naked, and the dress did the rest.

FITTED AND FITTING.

ONCE WHEN MILADY WANTED
A FROCK—

SHE WAS DULY MEASURED—

AND FITTED.

BUT NOW WHEN SHE SEES
A FROCK SHE FANCIES—

SHE UNDERGOES—

AN INTENSIVE COURSE OF SLIMMING—

IN THE BEAUTY DEPARTMENT—

AFTER WHICH—

SHE FITS *IT.*

The Government was astonished and disapproving of the New Look's popularity, arguing (not disinterestedly) that it relegated women to the status of caged birds. But it seems that after years of restrictions in the cause of austerity a few restrictions for the sake of elegance could be eagerly endured. At any rate, although the New Look itself was superseded after a season or two, cruelly pinching corsets were an inescapable fact of life for most women until well into the 1960s (Plate 63).

In the mid-1960s foundation garments became the exclusive preserve of the older generation, who continued to wear their reinforced bras and elastic girdles, while the young might wear no underwear at all, except perhaps two small pieces of sticking plaster to support the breasts. For the fashionable ideal now, more extreme than it had ever been, was Twiggy, who weighed $6\frac{1}{2}$ stone and had no more curves than a small child. And here the wheel comes full circle. Until the last twenty years or so, social historians have taken a stance of shocked incredulity at the folly of women who tight-laced; but in the 1970s, despite the well-

62   *29 February 1928*

"I'LL TELL YOU WHAT, OLD THING, THIS NEW FEMININE TOUCH IS ALL RIGHT, BUT YOU'LL HAVE TO ADOPT A NEW STANCE."

reasoned protests of feminists like Susie Orbach, we have seen a passion for slimming which knows no restraint. Anorexia nervosa has become increasingly common, and takes the same toll in health and life as tight-lacing ever did. This may partly explain why, in *Punch* nowadays, jokes about slimming are so scarce.

"*Actually, I only need **one** way*"

63   *24 January 1962*

3   The Poetry of Motion

'Well,' Laura began; then she stopped and spun round and round, for the strong wind blowing against her always made the wires of her hoop skirt creep slowly upward under her skirts until they bunched around her knees. Then she must whirl around and around until the wires shook loose and spiralled down to the bottom of her skirts where they should be.

As she and Carrie hurried on she began again. 'I think it was silly, the way they dressed when Ma was a girl, don't you? Drat this wind!' she exclaimed as the hoops began creeping upward again.

Quietly Carrie stood by while Laura whirled. 'I'm glad I'm not old enough to have to wear hoops,' she said. 'They'd make me dizzy.'

'They are rather a nuisance,' Laura admitted. 'But they are stylish, and when you're my age you'll want to be in style.'

Laura Ingalls Wilder, *Little Town on the Prairie*

It is one of the tensions of dress that while most of us believe that we choose our clothes largely with a view to comfort and practicality, few of us have not at some time or other suffered inconvenience, discomfort or even pain from one of our garments. It may have been shoes so pointed that they pinched the toes unmercifully; trousers so tight that walking was difficult and sitting down a major achievement; or foundation garments that cut cruelly into the flesh they were designed to contain. Whatever it may have been, we felt at that time a need to wear it which outweighed all considerations of comfort, for to know that one is wearing the right clothes affords, as one Edwardian lady expressed it, 'a peace of mind such as Religion cannot give'.

The wearing of clothes that impede free movement has generally been associated with Thorstein Veblen's theory of 'conspicuous leisure'. Certainly the medieval courtier whose shoes had such long points that they had to be held up by chains attached to his ankles was advertising the fact that he did not have to walk great distances. Similarly the stiff hooped skirts and full sleeves of wealthy Elizabethan ladies proclaimed their freedom from physical labour. In all ages the rich and fashionable have been able to afford impractical clothes, so that *Punch* shows us dandies whose high starched collars immobilize their heads (Plate 64), or whose gloves are so tight-fitting that they cannot flex their fingers without risking a split (Plate 65). This much is the continuation of a long tradition, a sense of the vulgarity of physical exertion taken to its logical conclusion. But a new and bewildering feature of the Victorian age was that however much a fashion may have been the creation of a leisured class, an expression of wealth and idleness, it did not remain so for long. In 1854 *Punch* gave vent to its irritation on the subject of sleeves, which were then being worn long, full and loose, in the style called 'pagoda':

64   *I, 1853, p. 58*   65   *17 January 1863*

X. 42. "Did you call the Police, Sir!"
Swell (who would perish rather than disturb his shirt-collar). "Ya—as, a—I've had the misfortune to dwop my Umbrellaw, and there isn't a boy within a mile to pick it up—a—Will you have the Goodness!"

Railway Official. "*Show your Ticket, Sir—please.*"
Swell. "*Haw, don't want to split my Gloves—would you be kyind enough to take it yourself out of my Waistcoat Pocket?*"

A WHOLESOME CONCLUSION.

Lady Crinoline. "YES, LOVE—A VERY PRETTY CHURCH, BUT THE DOOR IS CERTAINLY VERY NARROW!"

They are not only absurd but inconvenient. They are always getting in the way, and the sauce, and the butter-boat. Your wife cannot help you to a potato across the table but she upsets her glass, and breaks it with her dangling sleeve. It may be said that your wife has no business to help potatoes – that there ought to be footmen in attendance for that purpose. Certainly: or else, she should not wear the sleeves. But ladies must, of course, follow the height of fashion, whether suitable to their circumstances or not. Could not the leaders of fashion, then, in pity to the less opulent classes, devise and sanction a kind of sleeves adapted to life in a cottage – whether near a wood or elsewhere – to be called cottage sleeves, and to be worn by the genteel cottager-classes without prejudice to their gentility?

II, 1854, p. 109

But the first fashion to be universally adopted was the crinoline, and its exuberance was something unprecedented. Furthermore, it could be cheaply produced, and in no time at all every woman was wearing one. *Punch* had a wonderful time of it. Until then, bloomers had been the only article of dress to merit a full-scale attack, and that craze

THE SAFEST WAY OF TAKING A LADY DOWN TO DINNER.

67 *1 October 1864*

68 *2 October 1858*

NEW OMNIBUS REGULATION.

'Werry sorry 'm, but yer' l 'av to leave yer Krinerline outside."

had barely lasted six months. The crinoline stayed in vogue for eight years. For all that time *Punch* indulged in the wildest flights of fancy at its expense, occasionally sobering up to issue dire warnings about its dangers, but returning with obvious gusto to lampoons and send-ups. And there was plenty of justification for satire, for never has a fashion been so utterly impractical. It was bad enough for a lady of leisure: chairs, doorways (Plate 66), staircases (Plate 67), omnibuses (Plate 68) and theatre boxes all suddenly seemed too small; her children had difficulty in holding her hand, she could scarcely greet an acquaintance in the street (Plate 69), and shopping expeditions might prove hazardous. Thus *Punch*, at its most facetious:

MELANCHOLY ACCIDENT!!!

A Lady of Fashion incautiously walked up the Lowther Arcade last Tuesday afternoon. She quite forgot at the time that she was in full dress, and the consequences of her thoughtlessness have been most

69   *22 November 1856*

FRAGMENT OF AN UNPUBLISHED NOVEL OF FASHIONABLE LIFE.

deplorable. As the sails of her elegant but bulky costume flapped on either side of her, some object of *vertu* was swept remorselessly into oblivion. The Arcade in a few minutes presented a fearful wreck. The passage from one end to the other was strewn with sawdust and bear's-grease, rendered doubly dangerous by innumerable bits of glass. The extent of the damage may be estimated from the simple fact that it required not less than five carts to remove the broken fragments.

The following is the bill, which was presented, in all its horrible particulars, to her the following day:-

		£	s	d
25	*Noah's Arks – not one animal saved*	12	10	6
133	*China Cows, all destroyed, at 1s 1½ each*	7	6	3
33	*Prickly Porcelain Sheep*	0	15	6
240	*Pots of Pomatum, at 6d per pot*	6	0	0
57	*Bottles of Hair Oil*	2	5	6

70   10 August 1867

POSITIVELY THE LAST OF THE LONG SKIRTS THIS SEASON.

Hostess. "Oh, how Tiresome! Somebody must be Standing on my Dress! Would you just run Down-Stairs, and see who it is, Mr. Brown?"

		£	s	d
19	*Bottles of genuine Eau de Cologne (FARINA'S)*	0	9	6
10	*Children's Drums*	1	2	6
5	*Speaking Dolls, every one of whom has been bereft of speech*	6	1	6
3	*Pots of Blacking*	0	1	6
117	*Fly-Catchers*	2	1	6
41	*Panes of broken glass*	3	5	0
22	*Fire-grate Ornaments, perfectly soiled*	0	19	0
72	*Baa-lambs, the wool quite pulled off their backs*	3	19	6
35	*Musical Bow-wows, the bark of each literally pealed off*	2	7	6
1095	*Cups and Saucers, Soap Dishes, Powder Boxes, Wine-glasses, Tumblers (Bohemian and Brummagem), Ink-stands, Vases, Fish-globes, and Lamp Shades*	35	6	11
9	*Dolls' Houses, elegantly furnished, and all the furniture, pots and pans, broken to smithereens*	10	7	6
7	*Dolls' Four-post Bedsteads, with dolls in bed at the time*	5	8	9
3373	*Various other articles, far too numerous to mention, including Velvet Chimney Sweeps, Squirrel Nut-crackers, Swiss Chalets, Jenny Lind's Birthplaces, Stone-peaches, Wax-grapes, China Cheesecakes, Porcelain Candle-ends, Monk & Nun Extinguishers, Glass Save-alls, Albert Night-lights, Burns' Cottages, Musical Snuff-boxes, besides 133 Bellows, Accordions, Concertinas, and India-rubber Balls, in all of which the leather was found either pricked or cut – the entire amount having been estimated by the Editor of the* Economist *at*	273	18	8

		£374	7	1
Total				

16 August 1856

Far-fetched as this account may be, it is nevertheless true that one of the Staffordshire potteries lost in the course of a year £200 worth of goods knocked over by their employees' crinolines, and in 1860 Courtaulds had to issue a bill banning crinolines from the factory floor, where they got caught up in the machinery and caused serious accidents. For crinolines in working life were worse than inconvenient; they were positively dangerous. The worst hazard was fire. A skirt worn over several petticoats might smoulder if it came up against a flame, but there would be time to put it out before it actually blazed. But a skirt held out by a wire cage, affording plenty of ventilation underneath, could flare up in seconds and prove fatal to the wearer. Those most at risk were cooks, from their constant proximity to fires, and ladies who frequented balls, for their dresses were made of light and combustible fabrics which could easily catch in open grates or candle flames.

Magazines of the time offered numerous receipts for fireproofing fabrics, ranging from whitening and sal ammoniac to chloride of zinc and Epsom salts, but casualties were still frequent. *Punch* was shocked by the situation, but still could not help seeing the funny side. Many of the early crinolines consisted not of wires but of inflatable rubber tubes, which led *Punch* to make this suggestion:

> Fire-escapes should be provided in all drawing-rooms, by which ladies when alight might be rescued without scorching. As an additional precaution, the air-tubes of the petticoat might all be filled with water, and fitted with the means, when needful, to eject it. Every lady thus would, in fact, be her own fire-engine, and could play upon herself the moment her dress caught. At a moderate computation, a properly-spread petticoat contains some thousand feet of tubing; and such a reservoir as this would hold enough to put out any common-place conflagration.
>
> 8 January 1859

71   *20 February 1875*

PUTTING HIS FOOT IN IT.

Kate. "I'M AFRAID YOU'RE ENTANGLED!"
Augustus. "DON'T CARE, I'M SURE—IF YOU DON'T."

It was not only fire: children were swept off the edge of the pavement, skirts were caught up in passing cab-wheels, resulting in broken limbs, and on at least one occasion a high wind caused a woman to be blown off the promenade into the sea, an accident which prompted *Punch* to suggest that little boys might fly their sisters as kites.

No fashion before or since was as inconvenient as the crinoline, but the styles which succeeded it were still a far cry from simplicity or practicality. From the mid-1860s the fabric which had been evenly distributed over the hemispherical cage became increasingly drawn to the back of the figure, where it was arranged in ever more elaborate draperies. The crinoline itself shrank away in front, but remained at the back in the form of a bustle, from which the skirt fell into a train which dragged along the ground, causing no small inconvenience (Plates 70 and 71).

Crinoline at length is going out, thank goodness! but long, trailing dresses are coming in, thank badness! In matters of costume, lovely

72   *26 February 1876*

VETO.

"Shall we—a—sit down?"   "I should like to; but my Dressmaker says I mustn't!"

THE NEW HUSSAR HESSIANS AND PANTS.

" SEE, I 'VE DROPPED MY HANDKERCHIEF, CAPTAIN DE VERE!"
" I KNOW YOU HAVE, MISS CONSTANCE. I 'M VERY SORRY. I
AN'T STOOP, EITHER!"

73 *25 May 1878*

woman rarely ceases to make herself a nuisance; and the length of her skirt now is almost as annoying as, a while ago, its width was. . . . Everywhere you walk, your footsteps are impeded by the ladies, who, in POPE's phrase, 'drag their slow length along' the pathway just in front of you. 'Will anybody tread upon the tail of my petticoat?' This seems to be the general invitation they now give. Sad enemies to progress they are, in their long dresses: and a Reform Bill should be passed to make them hold their tails up. Ladies should be taught to mind their *p's* and *queues*; and every policeman should be armed with a big pair of garden shears or tailors' scissors, wherewith to cut away the skirts which he sees trailing on the pavement.

29 June 1865

As skirts became more tightly pulled across the front and more lavishly draped over the back, it became quite a feat for a woman to sit down (Plate 72), to go upstairs, or even to stoop. It is amusing to note

that military men of the period were undergoing the same constrictions
from their excessively tight trousers and boots (Plate 73). No wonder
that an announcement, in 1880, that 'short dresses are now good form in
the ball-room', was hailed with enthusiasm:

> All hail, Good Sense! Fair Reason, hail!
> Hail, Fashion's groaning slaves, set free
> From galling bonds of skirt and tail
> To revel in sweet liberty!
>
> Too long we've borne the foolish toils
> That Fashion weaves for each poor slave,
> Who, hampered with her monstrous coils,
> Has battled on, distraught but brave. . . .
>
> So, when the future ages scan
> The page of Fashion's folly dense,
> They shall confess *this* year began
> An era of sound Common Sense!

10 July 1880

HONESTY THE BEST POLICY.

Modest Youth. "MAY I HAVE THE PLEASURE OF DANCING WITH YOU, MISS LIGHTFOOT!"
Miss Lightfoot (to her *Mother's horror*). "THANKS—NO! MY WAISTBAND IS SO TIGHT I
CAN'T MOVE, AND SO ARE MY SHOES!"
[*Modest Youth, who is, let us say, an Earl of Richard the First's creation, six foot eight in his
pumps, with eight hundred thousand a year, and in every respect the ideal of a Young Girl's
Dream—is so touched that he proposes on the spot!*

74 *10 November 1883*

In point of fact common sense had to wait for another decade before gaining a foothold. Instead, the 1880s developed the bustle a stage further, so that instead of accentuating the natural lines of the female figure it stuck out at right angles to the back. It was claimed that you could balance a tea-tray on it, but curiously *Punch* produced no jokes about it – perhaps embarrassed that its predictions about common sense had been so wide of the mark. It did, however, pay tribute to a different brand of fashionable tyranny (Plate 74).

Impracticality is not a constant factor in dress, but occurs at random. Skirts did nothing more to incur public indignation or ridicule until 1910, when the craze for orientalism led to the universal adoption of the hobble skirt. This was undeniably difficult to walk in (Plate 75), and prompted many jokes. It threatened briefly to be revived in 1923 (Plate 76), but then, instead of lengthening, skirts rose to their shortest yet. Provided one did not mind showing one's legs, stocking-tops, garters and all, there was nothing awkward about the skirts of the 1920s – one could walk, bend or sit in them. By the 1930s, however, skirts had lengthened again, and the universal bias-cutting which wrapped the

75   *20 April 1910*

THE NEW SKIRT AND THE POETRY OF MOTION.

Edith (breaking into a hop). "Hurry up, Mabel; you 'll never catch the train if you keep on trying to run."

IN VIEW OF THE THREATENED RETURN OF THE "HOBBLE" SKIRT, THE MISSES BELMONT INTRODUCE AT THEIR TERPSICHOREAN STUDIO, A SPECIAL CLASS FOR GRACEFUL DEPORTMENT UNDER RESTRICTED CONDITIONS.

fabric tightly around the wearer produced much the same effect as the drapery of the 1870s (Plate 77).

Hats and fans might not wreak quite as much havoc as a full-blown crinoline, but clearly the very large fans carried in the early 1880s (Plate 78) and the sheaves of ostrich feathers of the early 1920s (Plate 79) could be quite a nuisance in theatre or ballroom. The 'flip-flop' hat which was part of the popular 'Dolly Varden' look of 1871 (named after the heroine of *Barnaby Rudge*, which was set in the 1780s, so that the fashion was in fact a revival of an eighteenth-century look) might only inconvenience its wearers (Plate 80). But in the mid-1890s there were many complaints about the size of women's hats, and they grew larger and more of a hindrance until well into the next century (Plate 81). Gwen Raverat remembered with feeling 'the torture of hats, the enormous over-trimmed hats, which were fixed to the armature of one's puffed-out hair by long and murderous pins. On the top of an open bus, in a wind, their mighty sails flapped agonizingly at their anchorage, and pulled out one's hair by the handful'. And *Punch* aired a common grievance in 'At the Private View':

> I'll see, I fear, not a picture here,
>   For ever there comes between
> A flower-bed on a lady's head –
>   That's pretty well all I've seen.

He. "SHALL WE—ER—*CAN* YOU—SIT DOWN?"

TIME PAST—CRINOLINE ERA.   **IN THE STALLS.**   TIME PRESENT—FAN DEVELOPMENT.

78   *12 August 1882*

> I dodge and dive, but I can't contrive
>   To peep past the things that trim
> That far from flat, waving, curling hat,
>   With its quite enormous brim.
>
> I'm short, she's tall, I can't see at all,
>   And she always comes between;
> Though quick or slow be my pace, no go,
>   In front she has ever been.
>
> So all I know of this picture show
>   Is a brim that scrapes my nose,
> On which upright, half a yard in height,
> Stands, 'blowing and growing', a rose.
>
> 12 May 189

Theatres had to issue printed requests to ladies to remove their hats
otherwise the stage would have been invisible to most of the audience
But even when taken off the hats could be a hazard. Sonia Keppel
remembered being taken to a matinée about Nero, in 1905:

> In the row of stalls behind us a lady arrived late. At that moment
> the stage was at its blackest and the thunder at its most loud.
> Blindly, she groped her way into her seat. Then she took the long
> pins out of her hat, removed her hat and pinned it to the back of the
> seat in front of her.

A scream, not from Agrippina, rang out by my side. On the stage the lightning flared, and by its light I beheld the terrifying spectacle of Sir Hedworth Williamson impaled, like a gigantic butterfly, on the back of his seat. And a doctor had to be sent for to dress the wound and to treat him for shock.

Throughout the nineteenth century there is a notable absence of allusions to the discomfort or inconvenience of men's clothes. This is doubtless due to the fact that *Punch*'s contributors were themselves men, and therefore disinclined to make jokes at their own expense. Dandies and aesthetes might be mocked, but they were a tiny minority who hardly impinged on most people's lives. The drawbacks of everyday male costume were accepted as inevitable. Towards the end of the century we find a solitary *cri de coeur* from an 'unwilling votary' of fashion:

79   *25 January 1922*

THE FAN PERIL.

Away from here, among the flowers,
　　By quiet country hedge-rows trim,
Would I might roam away the hours,
　　All unregarding Fashion's whim.
But throttled in her clutches grim,
　　I saunter stiffly down the Row –
Confound my collar's iron rim!
　　Il faut souffrir pour être beau.

I love to wander, head all bare,
　　On mountain fell, across the flat,
To feel the breezes kiss my hair,
　　Or storm-winds twine it in a mat.
But my poor head has Fashion gat
　　Fast in her vice, where'er I go –
Confound my thrice accurst top-hat!
　　Il faut souffrir pour être beau.

A 'social function' might have grace
　　But for the jostle and the squeeze,
The Park might be a pleasant place,
　　Could people dress as just they please.
If one might sit beneath the trees,
　　Bareheaded, flannelled, cool! – but no,
To slaves of Fashion farewell ease,
　　Il faut souffrir pour être beau.

Envoi

This truth comes borne with ball and rout,
　　At Lords, at Ascot, in the Row –
By night and day, in doors and out,
　　Il faut souffrir pour être beau.

20 June 1896

In 1925 the appearance of Oxford bags caused quite a stir, and their alleged impracticality prompted jokes similar to those about trained dresses (Plates 82 and 83), but it was not until 1931 that anyone was brave enough to look long and hard at men's evening dress and admit that it was uncomfortable, impractical and unattractive.

THE DOLLY VARDEN FAREWELL KISS.

A DELIGHTFUL OPERATION, BUT A DIFFICULT ONE TO PERFORM SUCCESSFULLY.

80   *14 October 1871*

SUNDERED LIVES.

Bertie. "I THOUGHT YOU TWO NEVER MET WITHOUT KISSING. ANYTHING THE MATTER? THE GREEN-EYED MONSTER?"
Muriel. "No, YOU SILLY! HATS!"

81   *6 July 1895*

In May, 1931, a party of Italian tourists, crossing the foot of the Mayfair Glacier (which covers, it will be remembered, the heart of ancient London), came upon the body of a man entombed in the ice. It was thought at first that this must be the victim of some recent holiday disaster; but the attention of the scientists was attracted by the extraordinary garments of the man; the body was carefully removed and the clothes 'preserved' by the Odo process, and yesterday at the Antiquarians' Annual Rally Dr. Prod announced hypotheses of a startling nature.

'There is little doubt', said the genial President, 'that a lucky chance has handed down to us the actual remains of a Briton of the early twentieth century, dressed in the most fantastic dress of that fantastic period. The body is that of one of the "upper" or "well-to-do" classes, as the rich were then described, and the clothes are those which would be worn in the evening or on holiday occasions. . . .'

So far from being simple, it appears to me to be one of the most complicated uniforms ever devised by man. I have made a careful analysis of the costume, piece by piece, and I find that it is made up of no fewer than twenty-five pieces, as follows:–

1 black coat or tunic.
1 white breast-plate.
1 white half-coat.
1 black leg-covering (?'trows').
2 pink under-garments.
1 white collar.
2 jewelled studs.
2 other studs.
2 cuff-links.
4 jewelled buttons.
2 socks.
2 suspenders (for above).
2 shoes.
1 elastic apparatus (attached to 'trows').
1 white necklet.

In addition there are fourteen buttons and two shoe-laces, which I have not included, as these, it seems, were permanently attached to the costume. Without them we are left with twenty-five pieces, which must have been assembled separately and carefully

82   *4 March 1925*

PERILS OF THE DANCE.
THE TERROR OF THE OXFORD TROUSERS.

fitted by the man or his servant whenever the dress was worn. By comparison the costume of a mediaeval knight was simple and spare, and the dressing of him an easy matter.

It is interesting again to compare this complicated dress with that of the Belgravia Woman, excavated a few years ago on the Cadogan Moraine and probably contemporaneous with the body we are now discussing. The costume of the Belgravia Woman, it will be remembered, consists of six pieces only . . . while the outer garment is of the utmost simplicity and could be put on and off in the twinkling of an eye. Compare with this the labours of the contemporary male, whose outer surface was made up of four distinct garments (not counting the collar, socks and shoes), and who before he could begin to dress at all must assemble and adjust a number of studs, buttons, ties, suspenders, braces, links and other small objects. . . . We can only begin to imagine the anxiety and patient labour which must have attended the putting on and wearing of this costume.

83   *1 April 1925*

MANNERS AND MODES.
CROSSING THE ROAD—1925.

What we are quite unable to understand is the attitude of the satirists of that time, who never wearied of poking fun at the clothes of women, but seem to have accepted as a matter of course the really laughable clothes of the men.

11 February 1931

Since the Second World War clothes have become more relaxed and informal. Starch is rarely used on men's shirts and suspenders have disappeared from their socks, while women's foundation garments have shrunk in both size and scope. But during the late 1950s and the early 1960s a new form of sartorial torture came in for both sexes, in the shape of Italian shoes. The crippling discomfort they caused was strikingly at variance with their cool, sophisticated image. Few people escaped their tyranny or can forget the pain of forcing their feet into an utterly unlikely shape. *Punch* provided a possible motivation:

LA DOLCE FEETA

Italy's shoes are like Italy's gents:
To foreign ladies, they give offence.
The shoe and the man initially please
But sinfully soon, they pinch and squeeze.

I hate those heels on the hoof, in the street.
Both make you suffer though each looks sweet.
I'll not be beguiled, despite their appeals:
As of today, I'm swearing off heels.

Unless, of course, a Don Juan comes by
Who likes me with heels impossibly high.
Then back to stilts, though the shoe abuses.
Life's short. Love's long – and worth a few bruises.

7 October 1964

The second half of the 1960s was the heyday of functionalism in dress, with its simple, uncluttered shapes, low-heeled shoes and practical fabrics like denim and PVC. Many people believed and forecast that fashion would never look back. But for generations practicality had been an also-ran among fashionable priorities. It was so now. The 1970s came up with floor-length skirts, murderously tight trousers, and platform shoes so high that the lead singer of Slade was rumoured to have broken his ankle by falling off his. And current street fashion has taken the whole business one stage further by divorcing clothes from any concept of practicality whatsoever. In the time and effort spent on creating a look which will be worn perhaps for only a few hours we see the full flowering of the decorative principle: clothes not as protection or even as attraction, but purely and simply as art.

4   New Bits to Show

The tendency to sexual display in dress is constantly at war with local and contemporary concepts of modesty, and consequently treads a precarious path. It must expose or emphasize parts of the body which are normally concealed, with sufficient boldness to attract or titillate, but not so shamelessly as to cause outrage or disgust. What is permissible varies according to time and place. Muslim women must hide their faces; Agnes Sorel exposed her breasts but never showed her legs, while flappers cut off their skirts at the knee but were well covered higher up; and many an English or American tourist has been angrily expelled from an Italian church when wearing shorts, a miniskirt or even a sleeveless dress, all of which would have been considered perfectly modest at home. Our own society takes a pragmatic approach to the question: provided the body looks good, the clothes cannot be bad, but to expose an ugly body more than absolutely necessary is indecent (Plates 84 and 85). As Edna Woolman Chase, *Vogue*'s formidable ex-editor, put it: 'Whether a Bikini bathing-suit on a charming young body is modest or immodest is a matter of the current mode or local morals or good taste; it has nothing to do with aestheticism. But too much revelation of a figure that is too thin, too fat, or too old can be lamentable.'

Over the centuries there has been considerable variety as to which parts of the body are emphasized. The medieval man of fashion padded his doublet to increase the size of his shoulders and chest, and wore it short enough to reveal his buttocks encased in tight hose, with the further embellishment of an ornate cod-piece, all stressing his aggressive masculinity. Historically women have not been allowed to emphasize their loins to the same extent, though the hip-hugging girdles of the Middle Ages, often descending to a point in front, and the sometimes suggestively positioned panels of beading on 1920s dresses might be cited as examples. Thus their breasts have more usually been the focus of

YOUNG HEADS UPON OLD SHOULDERS.

Enter Agnes. "O, HOW NICE AND COOL YOU MUST FEEL, GRANDMAMMA DEAR! WHY MAYN'T *I* WEAR A LOW BODY LIKE YOU AND AUNT METHUSELA?"

Grandmamma. "MY DEAR AGNES, WHAT NONSENSE! WHY, YOU'RE SCARCELY MORE THAN A MERE CHILD! YOU'D LOOK A PERFECT FRIGHT!"

84   *27 July 1872*

85   *28 October 1925*

Husband. "REALLY, LAURA, IF THESE SKIRTS GET ANY SHORTER THEY'LL BE HARDLY DECENT."

Wife. "MY DEAR MAN, DON'T YOU UNDERSTAND? ALL SKIRTS ARE DECENT, BUT NOT ALL LEGS."

"CHILDREN AND FOOLS SPEAK TRUTH."

Mamma. "Now, is there Anything Else I want?"
Alice (who has watched the toilet proceeding with interest and curiosity). "The Body, Mamma."

erotic attention. There is a story of two Regency men seeing a very décolletée lady at the theatre: 'Did you ever see such a thing?' – 'Not since I was weaned.' (The much publicized fashion of this time to wear one's light muslin dress wet so that it clung to every contour of the body is almost certainly apocryphal – for one thing the thin fabric would have dried out very quickly, making the effect disappointingly ephemeral.)

In the Victorian age two things happened. Men, having truly reached apotheosis in their relations with women, gave up dressing for any erotic purpose whatsoever, and women's dress became sharply contrasted between daytime and evening wear. Society was increasingly dominated by business, and during business hours frivolity was not permissible. Sex attraction was relegated to the status of spare-time interest. During the day, women were completely covered up. Skirts, of course, reached the ground, necks were high and sleeves came down to the wrist. Particularly at the beginning of our period, the whole form was enveloped, when out of doors, in a huge and shapeless shawl which blurred the figure, and the face was blinkered by a poke bonnet. Layers of petticoats and a rigid corset protected the wearer from contact with the world while producing the effect of doll-like fragility which was then in vogue. The evening was quite different:

"VAPID VEGETABLE LOVES."—" *The Talking Oak.*"
Scene—*Tea-Room at Fancy Ball.*

Uncle John (who is chaperoning his Niece). "What are you, my Dear?"
Pretty Niece. "Oh! I am a *Salad*, Uncle John! See, there's Endive, and
Lettuce, and Spring Onions, and Radishes, and Beetroot. Nothing wanting, is
there?"
Uncle John. "H'm!—ah!—perhaps a little more *Dressing*, my Dear!"

Emily. Shall you dress much to-night, dear?
Lilian. No - as little as possible - I am going to a ball.
9 October 1858

skirts still brushed the floor, but the top half of the body was suddenly
exposed. Hair was no longer hidden under caps or bonnets, but
embellished with ribbons, lace and flowers; sleeves were short, and
bodices (known as 'bodies') were cut extremely low (Plate 86). The
contrast must have been most effective, but inevitably there were those
who found fault with it. *Punch*, hailing a statement in the fashion
magazine *Le Follet* that 'the dress is not worn so low as last year, either on
the back or front', remarked:

It sadly lowers one's opinion of the sense of the fair sex to consider
that, with many women, modesty is nowadays a matter of mere
fashion. For many a month past dresses have been worn so low as
barely to be decent. Ladies who of late have been modestly attired,
could lay no claim whatever to being in the fashion. Decency,
however, is once more to be the *mode*, and, as few ladies have the

courage to disobey their dressmakers, we may hope that for a while, until the fashion changes, we may be able to dine out, and even go to dances, without blushing for our partners.

11 April 1868

Clearly decency failed to establish itself, for two years later *Punch* was complaining once again, and once more quoting from a fashion magazine. (It is amusing to note that *Punch*, while considering itself vastly superior to feminine preoccupations, clearly spent a lot of time looking through fashion magazines in search of suitable copy.)

'The low square cut corsage now in vogue, which has come to be disrespectfully styled the *étalage*, consists of little else than a mere band of cerise velvet, bordered above and below with blonde lace, which with a rose posed at each shoulder suffices to form the sleeves.'

What is called full dress is often barely decent, and ladies when most dressed have commonly least clothing. They who practise such exposure as is hinted at above deserve to be exposed to the severest form of censure. It is not enough to say that they are barefaced, for it is not their face which is the front of their offending. A cut at them in Punch is castigation they well merit; but were Punch to represent such women as they are, and as they ought not to be, Punch might cease to be regarded as a decent publication. Want of decency, the poet says, is want of sense; and no one but a fool would deem herself dressed properly, with a shred of lace, two roses, and a little scrap of velvet.

30 April 1870

Dresses undoubtedly were revealing (Plate 87); but, as long as the contrast between day and evening wear was maintained, they did not cease to make an impact, and any part of the body – such as the arms – which was now muffled up and now totally exposed, could and did become charged with erotic power.

Stephen was mute: he was incapable of putting a sentence together, and Maggie bent her arm a little upward towards the large half-opened rose that had attracted her. Who has not felt the beauty of a woman's arm? – the unspeakable suggestions of tenderness that lie in the dimpled elbow, and all the varied gently-lessening curves down to the delicate wrist, with its tiniest, almost

THINGS ONE WOULD RATHER HAVE EXPRESSED DIFFERENTLY.

She. "I'm surprised to see your Wife in such a *very* Low Gown this cold evening, Baron! I heard she was Delicate."
He. "Ach, no! She vos. But now, sank Heafen, she is kvite *In*delicate again!"

88   *6 April 1895*
89   *11 May 1904*

FIRST IMPRESSIONS.

Father. "Why, what a little Woman she's getting!"
Mother. "Yes, a very expensive young Lady. She grows out of all her Frocks."
Dorothy. "Mamma's expensive too. She's grows out of her Pretty Frock!"

imperceptible nicks in the firm softness. . . . A mad impulse seized
on Stephen: he darted towards the arm, and showered kisses on it,
clasping the wrist.

George Eliot, *The Mill on the Floss*

As the century progressed, and long white evening gloves became *de
rigueur*, the emphasis shifted to a back and front décolleté, which was set
off by the very large puffed sleeves of the 1890s (Plate 88) and which, by
the turn of the century, had slipped down to reveal the whole of the
shoulders as well as a substantial quantity of bosom, giving the wholly
calculated impression that at any minute the entire dress might drop to
the ground (Plate 89). The heroine of Dorothy Canfield's *The Bent Twig*,
dressing for a society dinner in a self-made gown,

> . . . settled on her slim, delicately modeled shoulders the straps of
> shirred and beaded chiffon which apparently performed the office
> of keeping her dress from sliding to the floor. In reality, under its
> fluid, gauzy draperies, it was constructed on a firm, well-fitting,
> well-fastened foundation of opaque cloth which quite adequately
> clothed the young body, but its appearance was of a transparent
> cloud, only kept from floating entirely away by those gleaming
> straps on the shoulders, an effect carefully calculated in the original
> model, and inimitably caught by Sylvia's innocent fingers.

On the point of going downstairs, however,

> . . . she was halted by an inexplicable hesitation about opening the
> door and showing herself. She looked down at her bare shoulders
> and bosom, and faintly blushed. It was really very, very low, far
> lower than any dress she had ever worn! And the fact that Eleanor
> Hubert, that all the 'swell' girls, wore theirs low, did not for the
> moment suffice her – it was somehow different – their showing their
> shoulders and her showing her own. . . . Finally she compromised
> by picking up a pretty spangled scarf Aunt Victoria had sent her,
> wrapping it about her like a shawl, in which quaint garb she went
> out in more confidence, and walked down the hall to the stairway.

In England parents exerted more control over their daughters'
clothes than in America, where Sylvia could dress as she pleased; and
young girls were not permitted the same degree of exposure as their
mothers. When Sonia Keppel was presented at Court immediately after

he First World War, she remembers that 'to the envy of my girl-friends,
Mr Reville prevailed on Mamma to let me have hardly any sleeves. Up
ill then, we all had draped bits of net, or chiffon, or the stuff the dress
was made of, concealing the outlines of our shoulders'. But although she
regarded this as an unexpected parental indulgence, the aftermath of
he war was also a significant factor. The general mood was one of
reckless gaiety and a widespread flouting of the old order. Women's
evening dress became skimpier than ever before (Plate 90), and clothes
which had once been the prerogative of chorus girls became quite
respectable (Plates 91 and 92). Bosoms and shoulders were still bared,
but now legs too were visible. Fleur Mont, in Galsworthy's *Silver Spoon*,
'was returning downstairs from showing the young man to his room.
Already fully dressed for the evening, she had but little on' (Plate 93).
The sight of all this nudity prompted *Punch* to address 'Julia, in Envy of
Her Toughness':

90   *25 June 1919*

" I 'M TOLD SHE 'S ALWAYS WRITING TO HER DRESSMAKER ABOUT NEW FROCKS."
" I SUPPOSE SHE ENCLOSED A STAMPED AND ADDRESSED ENVELOPE FOR THAT ONE."

When I, in this revolting weather,
    As served throughout the Arctic zone,
Just keep my soul and flesh together
    By wearing things that weigh a stone,
And find that you go undefeated
    In clothes that let the blast blow through,
I marvel why my sex is treated
    As much the tougher of the two.

When Earth is wrapped in frosty vapour
    And barren boughs with snow are fledged,
Your callous legs still love to caper
    In summer hose of silk (alleged);
While I, if thus I mocked the blizzard
    Or rashly dared the bitter rime –
I should be stricken in the gizzard,
    I should be dead in three days' time.

Having survived the day's exposure
    At eve you bare your hardy spine,
Marking that exhibition's closure
    At well below the old waist-line;
This seems to cause your lungs no trouble,
    Yet if I danced *sans* shirt and vest
I should incur pneumonia (double)
    And in a week or so go West.

How comes it you enjoy a measure
    Of nudity to me denied?
Is it because your frame, my treasure,
    Is coated with a coarser hide?
I fear you'll deem this view abhorrent,
    So let me add, to break the blow,
You are – and will remain, I warrant –
    The nicest pachyderm I know.

9th December 192⁵

With increasing exposure of the body, and with the related cults o
health and slimming, a perfect figure began to be more important than a
pretty face. The bare shoulders and arms of the Victorian age had neve
significantly distracted attention from the face, but bare legs meant tha
glances were concentrated lower down (Plate 94), a fact which wa

MANNERS AND MODES.

HORRIBLE NIGHTMARE OF A LADY WHO DREAMS THAT SHE HAS GONE TO A BALL IN HER NIGHT-GOWN
AND FOUND HERSELF SHOCKINGLY OVERDRESSED.

91　*7 January 1920*

acknowledged when hemlines dropped again at the end of the 1920s
(Plate 95). With legs covered up once more, the emphasis moved to the
back, which was totally bared (Plate 96), and, as skirts were bias-cut and
very close-fitting, the effect was rather like that of a mermaid. Between
the end of the war and the middle of the 1930s, almost every part of the
body had been displayed and withdrawn in turn (Plate 97).

Throughout the 1950s and 1960s there was a return to a more
classically feminine, generously proportioned figure modelled on Marilyn
Monroe and Jayne Mansfield, and the erotic emphasis was on the breasts,
uplifted, padded if need be, and shown off by tightfitting sweaters in the
daytime and by plunging necklines at night (Plate 98). Despite brief
flourishes of competition, such as were presented by bare midriffs, the
bosom's supremacy remained unchallenged until the mid-1960s, when it

Old-fashioned Aunt. "GOOD HEAVENS, CHILD! YOU'RE NOT GOING OUT LIKE THAT? YOU LOOK LIKE A CHORUS-GIRL."
Modern Maiden. "OH, COME, AUNT! I DON'T LOOK AS HORRIBLY RESPECTABLE AS THAT, SURELY?"

92 *11 February 1920*   **93** *12 May 1926*

Girl (who is eating an apple). "I FEEL LIKE EVE."
Companion. "OH, I DON'T KNOW. SEVERAL WOMEN HERE AREN'T CLOTHED ANY MORE THAN YOU."

Husband. " I SHOULD HAVE THOUGHT YOU 'D BE ASHAMED TO SHOW YOUR FACE IN SUCH A GOWN."
Wife. " DON'T WORRY, DARLING. MY FACE WON'T BE THE CHIEF ATTRACTION."

94   *16 January 1929*

indulged a final fling in the form of total exposure – the topless look (Plate 99). Meanwhile skirts were climbing above the knee. In 1968, those who wanted the best of both worlds could buy a minidress with a see-through top; but by this time breasts had substantially lost their erotic appeal and were used instead as shock tactics in the generation war. The girl of the swinging sixties abolished her bust just as effectively as the flapper of the 1920s, cropped her hair just as boyishly, and aspired to long, thin legs, which were frequently clothed in boots, or vividly patterned and textured tights which could not fail to command attention.

As skirts rose higher and higher the erotic focus rose too, until in the late 1960s Mary Quant identified the crotch as the new erogenous zone, and proved it by having her pubic hair shaved into a heart shape. This widely publicized action had in fact been anticipated almost forty-five years earlier by Eric Gill in a rhyme which he accompanied by a graphic, if stylized, drawing:

> If skirts get any shorter
> Said the flapper with a sob
> There'll be two more cheeks to powder
> And one more place to 'bob'.

95   *25 February 1931*

96   *30 May 1934*

"I'M GETTING TO LIKE THIS RETURN TO LONG SKIRTS. I FIND IT REVIVES MY MEMORY FOR FACES."

"REALLY, MY DEAR, YOU LOOK AS IF YOU WERE WEARING YOUR SUN-BATHING DRESS."
"I AM, UNCLE DARLING. I CAN'T AFFORD A NEW FROCK AND I HATE LOOKING CONSPICUOUS."

Many skirts were indeed quite short enough to reveal 'all', particularly when the wearers stretched or stooped, and the advent of tights, while eliminating the sight of stocking-tops and suspenders, led many girls to dispense with knickers, thus increasing sexual tension in many work situations. Where trousers were worn, they were tight around the hips and thighs.

The fall of the miniskirt was not hastened by any rival attraction. During the 1960s exposure itself was over-exposed and fashion took refuge in the demure look epitomized by Laura Ashley: high necks, long sleeves and floor-length skirts. This moratorium on blatant sexual display perhaps explains male mourning for the mini (Plate 100).

And the men themselves, sizing up legs and appraising bosoms, what have they offered? We saw that in the Victorian age men dressed to express their competence in business, not to attract women (the women gravitated to them anyway, having no alternative); thus the whole idea of sexual display is seen as an absurdity (Plate 101). Even the upheaval of the Great War and the anything-goes mood of the 1920s failed to shake

97 *11 July 1934*

"WELL I NEVER, MUMMY! IS THAT YOUR NEW DRESS? HOWEVER DO YOU MANAGE TO THINK OF NEW BITS TO SHOW?"

"*Why not? You're flaunting **your** secondary sexual characteristics.*"

98   *21 October 1964*

99   *8 July 1964*

"*We should be going in a couple of minutes — You're
nowhere near ready, I hope.*"

he Englishman's paradoxical conviction that dressing conspicuously in order to attract women was effeminate. It was not until after the Second World War that the influence of American gangster movies produced, among the young, a fashion for aggressively masculine clothes, loosely draped suits and padded shoulders which would not have disgraced Henry VIII, and which were undoubtedly a form of erotic display (Plate 102). This trend persisted but was, and still substantially is, confined to the young. See-through shirts, or ones worn open to the waist, the (preferably) hairy chest further emphasized by a pendant, enjoyed a vogue in the 1960s, and tight trousers had a long innings (Plate 103). In 1969 John Taylor, the editor of *Tailor and Cutter*, remarked in *Punch* that the tight trousers of the younger generation nowadays . . . are quite as revealing as the buckskin breeches of the past "physical" era – the Regency – and earlier times when the bulge of the private parts was not so much concealed by the cod-piece as emphasised' (19 March 1969). And the following year Anthony Price designed a pair of trousers with an appliqué hand reaching up and over the crotch. At this time, too, it

00   *4 November 1970*

"One can only hope that under every maxi there is a mini skirt trying to get out."

101 *16 August 1879*

A DANGEROUS RIVAL.

Fashionable Wife. "GOOD HEAVENS, GEORGE! YOU ARE NOT GOING TO
DINNER LIKE THAT!!"

Athletic Husband. "JUST *AIN'T* I THOUGH! LOOK HERE, MARIA, I'LL GRANT
YOU YOUR NECK AND SHOULDERS, AND YOUR PRETTY FACE; BUT I *THINK* I
BEAT YOU IN THE MATTER OF ARMS—AND IF SO, WHY SHOULDN'T I SHOW AS
MUCH OF THEM AS YOU DO?"

102 *10 May 1948*

103 *2 June 1965*

was well known that tight-trousered pop singers, gyrating before large audiences, supplemented the deficiencies of nature with lengths of rubber hose.

We are now in a different phase. Most people over a certain age still have very traditional views of what is sexually attractive – broad shoulders and lean hips for men, and a trim but curvaceous figure emphasized by well-fitting clothes for women – but many younger people reject these stereotypes. If they do conform to them, they do so with tongue in cheek, as another way of dressing up, but they are just as likely to adopt a completely androgynous look. Their clothes seem to say that they are at liberty to attract each other by physical or other means, or not to bother. Thus sexual attraction has become a matter of individual taste and not of convention.

5 The Way to Wareham

Local and temporary customs in dress have frequently been enforced in the name of modesty or decency, as though these were unchanging moral absolutes, only to be ousted with derision in another time or place; but only the wearing of trousers by women has been denounced on the highest moral and religious grounds as contrary to God's will, and this for centuries on end. For hundreds of years women in our civilization wore long skirts while men wore trousers, and to step out of line was to court swift and certain retribution. It was one of the gravest charges brought against Joan of Arc that she had dared to adopt breeches, and the obvious common sense of her choice did not weigh at all against its impropriety. This traditional allocation of dress was deemed un-assailable on the authority of the Bible, which ruled that 'a woman must not wear men's clothes nor a man put on women's dress; anyone who does this is detestable to Yahweh your God' (an allusion to certain practices in Canaanite religions). Nowhere, however, did the Bible state that women might not wear trousers as such. It is clear that, in the course of time, trousers had ceased to be merely a kind of garment worn by men, and had become the most powerful symbol of manhood. Thus the woman who wore them was not simply pursuing practicality or variety, but was usurping man's superior role. Since this was felt intolerable, she was charged with immodesty and blasphemy.

In medieval times, women did not even wear drawers: one of the stories in the *Book of the Knight of the Tower* hinges on this fact. Later on, Renaissance courtesans in Italy wore dresses with loose panels which could be lifted to reveal breeches underneath – a sure sign of their profession. Drawers were not common until the nineteenth century, and the crinoline was partly responsible for their adoption. Skirts worn over a number of heavy petticoats stayed in their place, but one stretched over a light wire cage was liable to fly into the air as the result of exertion or gusts of wind, so drawers were necessary to modesty. But even then

WOMAN'S EMANCIPATION.

(Being a Letter addressed to Mr. Punch, with a Drawing, by a strong-minded American Woman.)

BLOOMERISM—AN AMERICAN CUSTOM.

they were considered highly indelicate – as much so as what they concealed. The young Duchess of Manchester tripped over a stile during an energetic paperchase and landed with her skirts above her head. She was wearing scarlet tartan knickerbockers, of which the Duc de Malakoff got a good view – 'C'était diabolique', he commented – but significantly the other ladies in the party hardly knew whether to be glad or not that she was wearing them. For years drawers were pictured in advertisements discreetly folded.

The first consistent attempt at female trouser-wearing came from America and was inextricably linked with the incipient movement for women's rights. American women suffered the same inequality in law as their English sisters, but in practice they were very much more emancipated, which made them more articulate in their demands for equal rights. They had toiled beside their husbands to civilize the new land, they had faced every danger, suffered every privation and assumed every responsibility. Having no concept of the vulgarity of work, they were far more active in the domestic line than English women. Their long skirts were a constant impediment to them, and they wanted to get rid of them. Mrs Bloomer is commonly credited with inventing the 'bloomer' costume: it was in fact the brainchild of Libby Smith. Libby's father was broad-minded and progressive. He considered that while women wore cumbersome and crippling clothes they would always be treated like slaves, and he brought up his daughter very freely, allowing her to romp and play like a boy and to dress as she pleased. In 1850 she married Charles Dudley Miller, and while in Switzerland on her honeymoon she made herself an outfit modelled on the clothes worn in Swiss sanatoriums by women recovering from the effects of tight-lacing. This costume comprised a skirt reaching to just below the knee, worn over long, full, Turkish trousers. Out of doors, she added a cloak, furs and a beaver hat. Her husband thoroughly approved of this unconventional get-up and stoutly defended her against all criticism. Dressed like this, Libby came to stay with her cousin, Elizabeth Cady Stanton, in the little New York town of Seneca Falls.

Elizabeth Cady Stanton was already active in the women's movement, but she had not yet gone over to the idea of wearing men's costume. Indeed she had written that such an idea was 'in violation of every principle of duty, taste and dignity', and admitted an admiration for the 'easy graceful folds' of women's dress. But when she saw Libby 'with a lamp in one hand and the latest Stanton baby in the other, walk upstairs with ease and grace, whilst she with flowing robes pulled herself up with difficulty, carrying only a can of hot water', she became convinced that there was a pressing need for reform in women's dress. She adopted the trouser costume, and experienced an overwhelming sense of freedom. Amelia Jenks Bloomer, her friend, neighbour and fellow feminist, was the next to follow suit, though more out of feminist solidarity than personal preference. Because she was the editor of the feminist magazine *The Lily* and publicized the new costume in its pages, she received all the credit for it, gave her name to the outfit, and became a celebrity overnight. For the costume was a great success. *The Lily* was deluged with requests for details and patterns, and bloomers were worn on all sorts of occasions, even at a ball. On the whole the American press was favourable, considering it a highly attractive get-up, but the clerical establishment was predictably hostile and thundered against the bloomer as contrary to the dictates of Moses. Mrs Bloomer was, however, equal to every criticism. Was there anything in the Bible, she demanded, to suggest that Adam's figleaf apron differed from Eve's?

'With all the history of male and female attire before him, and with so much proof of the similarity in dress, how can Mr Talmage [one

106   *II, 1851, p. 160*   107   *II, 1851, p. 184*

APROPOS OF BLOOMERISM.

No. 1. *(who is looking at the Print of the Bloomer Costume).* "WELL, NOW, UPON MY WORD, DON'T SEE ANYTHING RIDICULOUS IN IT. I SHALL CERTAINLY ADOPT IT."
No. 2. "FOR MY PART, I SO THOROUGHLY DESPISE CONVENTIONALITY, THAT I HAVE ORDERED ALL MY NEW THINGS TO BE MADE IN THAT VERY RATIONAL STYLE!"

BLOOMERISM IN A BALL-ROOM.

Bloomer. "MAY I HAVE THE PLEASURE OF DANCING THE NEXT POLKA WITH YOU?"

of her critics] set up the claim that men have a right to any
particular style, and that if women dare to approach that style they
break divine law and commit great sin and wrong? It is a
presumption and insult which women everywhere should resent.

Moses, she added slyly, had instructed men to put fringes and blue
ribbons on their garments – where were Mr Talmage's?
   News of bloomers first reached England on 31 May 1851, when *The
Times*, under the heading 'A Lady Resolved to Be Free and Easy'
quoted some of Amelia's writings from *The Lily*. Then, a couple of
months later, the *Illustrated London News* printed a picture of Amelia and
an article headed 'The American Ladies' New Costume', and *Punch*
published a satirical drawing (Plate 104) and a letter entitled 'Woman's
Emancipation', supposedly written by a 'strong-minded American
Woman' called Theodosia Eudoxia Bang. As one might expect, the
drawing is a highly inaccurate portrayal of the bloomer costume, and

108   *II, 1851, p. 192*

ONE OF THE DELIGHTFUL RESULTS OF BLOOMERISM.—THE LADIES WILL
POP THE QUESTION.

Superior Creature. "SAY! OH, SAY, DEAREST! WILL YOU BE MINE?" &c., &c.

A POSER FOR A BLOOMER.

Old Gentleman. "Before I can Entertain your Proposal, and Give my Consent to your Marrying my Son, I must ask you, Whether you are in a Position—a—to—a—Keep him in the Style to which—a—I may say—He has always been Accustomed? Ahem!"

109   II, 1851, p. 208

he text seems sadly unfunny, though doubtless it succeeded well enough n amusing its Victorian male readers.

A few weeks later *Punch* returned to the attack with a supposed etter from Mrs Bloomer to the female race. It is written in the usual hotchpotch of capitals, italics, dashes and emotional language which *Punch* considered typical of female writers.

Such is the *timid virgin*, who would be a – *Bloomer*!

See her in plumage *for her first flight*! She trips in her *boudoir* in dread and fear. She looks from the window – *her* nest – into the street! With *a beating heart* she trips down stairs – the street-door stands open! There – there on the other side of the threshold – is a *cold*, a *tyrannous*, a *hungry*, and *insulting* world! This *she knows*; and, if she has the *true soul* of a woman – of a woman fit for *the future destiny* of her sex – she *throws down the guage* [*sic*], for she crosses the *door-step*!

The Young Bloomer is *in the street*!

II, 1851, p. 128

And so on for two columns.

Next came a full-page drawing of two American Bloomerites (Plate 105), both looking suitably strong-minded, both smoking cigars (a

practice connected with bloomerism only in the public fancy), being
hooted at by urchins in the street and shunned with dismay and disdain
by a pair of virtuous British matrons.

So far it was only reports of strange happenings across the Atlantic
but a British Association of Bloomers was formed, and in September
1851 *The Times* reported that two young and two older women had go
out of a cab and distributed handbills 'containing a spirited appeal to
the women of England to throw off the yoke of their unfeeling and brutal
oppressors, and adopt an attire better suited to the dignity of the equal of
man'. The women were surrounded by a laughing and cheering crowd
and soon hailed another cab to make their escape. More pioneers
ventured on to the London streets, and a lecture was announced to be
given by a Mrs C. Dexter of America. The room was filled to
overflowing by a boisterous crowd, but the speaker presumably lost her
nerve, for the lecture was postponed until the following week, to the
considerable indignation of the crowd. When the lecture eventually
took place it featured twenty bloomered ladies sitting on the stage
though their reception was such that two of them had to retire in order to

BLOOMERISM!

Strong-Minded Female. "Now, do, pray, Alfred, put down that Foolish Novel
and do Something Rational. Go and play Something on the Piano; you never
Practise, now you're Married."

NOSCE TEIPSUM.
Lady Cyclist (touring in North Holland). " What a Ridiculous Costume ! "

regain their composure. Despite all these setbacks, the speaker was rewarded with 'unanimous acclamation'.

The theatre was quick to exploit the new costume and many plays featured it. *A Figure of Fun, or the Bloomer Costume, Bloomerism, or the Follies of the Day* – the titles indicate the general public's attitude to the proposed dress reform. It was never taken seriously in England, where the women's rights movement barely existed yet. Even its critics had to admit that it had health and hygiene on its side, but they felt that these advantages were overridden by a fundamental impropriety. Thus *Punch*, parodying Thomas Carlyle:

A praiseworthy point in Bloomerism the emancipation of the ribs: an exceeding good riddance the deliverance from corset, trammel-ling genteel thorax with springs of steel and whalebone, screwing in waist to Death's hour-glass contraction, and squeezing lungs, liver and midriff into an unutterable cram. Commendable, too, the renouncement of sous-jupe bouffante, or ineffable wadding, invented, I suppose, by some Hottentot to improve female contour after the type of VENUS, his fatherland's, and not Cythera's. Wholesome, moreover, and convenient, the abbreviation of trains, serving in customary female Old Clothes the purpose of besom, and no other: real improvements, doubtless, these abandonments

IN DORSETSHIRE.

Fair Cyclist. "Is this the way to Wareham, please?"   *Native.* "Yes, Miss, yew seem to me to ha' got 'em on all right!"

of ruinous shams, ridiculous unveracities, and idolatries of indescribable mud-Pythons. But Bloomerist inexpressible affectations, and mimicries of masculine garments, nether and upper, such, my friends, I take to be no more than dumb, inarticulate clamourings for the Rights of Women, GEORGE SAND phantasms, and mutinous female radicalisms grown termagant and transcendent.

II, 1851, p. 217

In the England of 1851 anything which smacked of feminism was certain to be met with ridicule. It is significant that although Amelia Bloomer, Elizabeth Cady Stanton and Libby Smith were all young, attractive married women, the British press invariably portrayed them, and often their followers, as ugly frustrated spinsters (Plate 106). Further jokes on the subject were not really concerned with bloomers as such, but used them as a pretext for humorous role reversal: how hilarious if girls were to ask young men to dance (Plate 107), let alone if they should propose to them (Plates 108 and 109), or assume a position of authority (Plate 110)!

Bloomerism lasted barely six months in England, and in that short time it is doubtful if many women were brave enough to follow it. *Punch* gives a false impression: the number of jokes on the subject reflects not the popularity of the fashion but the absurd light in which it was seen by the public. In America it survived slightly longer, but the women who had first worn it decided that the kind of publicity it attracted was no longer useful to the women's cause. They were none of them by nature exhibitionist, and it was with some relief that they gradually returned to less conspicuous dress.

No more was heard of trousers for women for some forty years, but in that time social attitudes gradually changed. Women were still a long way from equality, or even the vote, but their sphere of activity was slowly increasing; the popular heroines of fiction were no longer modest violets shrinking from the coarser sex, but often lively and energetic. From croquet in the crinolines of the 1860s women had progressed to lawn tennis in the 1870s and 1880s, and in the 1890s cycling was all the rage. Naturally this form of sport demanded a suitable get-up, and knickerbockers enjoyed quite a vogue. The cycling knickerbocker made no claims beyond that of practicality; it was not linked to a programme of social reform, nor did it symbolize feminism. As a result, although it was teased, it was never attacked or lampooned as savagely as bloomers had been, and its wearers were usually depicted as young and attractive (Plates 111 and 112). The prevailing attitude was summed up in *Punch*'s poem entitled 'Herrick on Rational Dress':

> . . . I will not say I wholly *like*
> To see my JULIA on a 'bike':
> I will not say that I should *choose*
> To see CORINNA don the trews;
> But yet, if either beauty feel
> That she is *bound* to cycle-wheel,
> (Like to a she-Ixion) then,
> Since ladies aim to ride like men,
> 'Tis clear that all experience teaches
> That it is best to wear knee-breeches,
> And drop the prejudice that doth dote
> On the tempestuous petticoat. . . .
> Knickers and leggings, by-and-by,
> With their unfeigned simplicity,
> Will more bewitch us – on a 'bike' –
> Than flowing skirts we now do like!
>   29 September 1894

She dressed herself in the latest mode,
And left her house in the Brompton Road,

To popularise the harem kit,
But she found that nobody noticed it.

And the ribald laughter she hoped to hear
Never assailed her wakeful ear.

So she gave a street-boy twopence to scoff,
But, just as the urchin was starting off,

A scandalized constable made a grab—
And home she went in a taxi-cab.

And, being fed up with the whole affair,
Adapted the thing for her husband's wear.

Shortly after this poem appeared, an account of a lady cyclist in knickerbockers being hissed at in the street by an 'elderly Mrs Grundy' prompted *Punch* to a vigorous defence of the new rational dress. It takes the form of a dialogue between a Proud Briton and a Perfect Stranger, in which the former tries to explain that any degree of impropriety is socially acceptable so long as it is neither new nor unexpected, while anything out of the ordinary is considered subversive of the accepted social laws, and therefore merits the Matron's Hiss.

'Then', commented the Perfect Stranger, 'the Matron's Hiss would be silent at the sight of bared shoulders and bust in midwinter, but would sound with anserine shrillness at the sight of a lady's lower limbs comfortably, and conveniently, and healthily, *and* decently, but unconventionally, clad in summer on a cycle?'

'Precisely!' said the Proud Briton, though perhaps with less of British pride than usual.

'Then,' said the Perfect Stranger, 'I think your Hissing

Taxi-driver (who has received bare legal fare, to Lady Maud, on munitions). "'ERE, WOT'S THIS? CALLS YERSELF A GENTLEMAN, DO YER?"

OUR LAND-WORKERS.

Mabel (discussing a turn for the village Red Cross Concert). "WHAT ABOUT GETTING OURSELVES UP AS GIRLS?"
Ethel. "YES—BUT HAVE WE THE CLOTHES FOR IT?"

115 *31 January 1917*

Matron is a silly, despotic, cackling old goose, who will never save the social Capitol!'

13 October 1894

By a curious irony, it was at the height of the knickerbocker craze that news was received of Mrs Bloomer's death in Iowa. It would seem that *Punch* repented its savage attacks of the past and, while still considering her costume without favour, was prepared to accord her a not ungenerous epitaph:

> So MRS BLOOMER's gone! but let her name
> Once more appear in *Mr. Punch*'s pages.
> 'Twas long ago, almost the Middle Ages,
> That LEECH's pencil advertised her fame!
>
> Her costume was unlovely – let it fade
> For ever from the ken of human vision!
> Though nowadays 'twould scarce provoke derision,
> If worn by pretty girls and tailor-made.

For by the lady-cyclist, as she plies
  Her pedal, neatly clad in knickerbockers,
  See MRS BLOOMER, first of Grundy-shockers,
Now vindicated in Dame Fashion's eyes!

But, not in dress alone a pioneer,
  She edited the temp'rance *Water Bucket*,
  And many a blow 'gainst drink with pluck hit;
Then let us o'er her passing shed a tear!

26 January 1895

Trousers made a brief reappearance for everyday wear in the years immediately before the Great War, when the two major influences on fashion were Paul Poiret and the Russian Ballet. Between them they promoted a passion for orientalism, as a result of which anything exotic was eagerly sought after. From the bell-shaped, frilled extravaganzas of the Edwardian age, skirts became narrow to the point of restricting movement (the hobble skirt), and bold leaders of fashion adopted harem trousers. It is doubtful if this fashion was ever widespread; we read of wearers being chased off the streets, but *Punch* is eager to convey the opposite impression, that is to say that nobody was interested enough to

116   *14 March 1917*

THE SCARECROW.

TROUSERS FOR WOMEN ARE NOT NECESSARILY UNATTRACTIVE. THEY CAN BE QUITE BECOMING IN THE FORM OF—

A SMOKING SUIT—

AND FOR SPORTS WEAR THEY ARE
NOT UNREASONABLE;

BUT SHOULD THEY BE ADOPTED IN
THE CITY—

IN THE DOMESTIC CIRCLE—

AT ASCOT—

FOR DINNER-PARTIES—

OR IN THE BALLROOM—

OLD-FASHIONED PEOPLE MAY REGRET
THE MORE MAIDENLY FASHIONS OF
TO-DAY—

OR EVEN THOSE OF A DOZEN
YEARS AGO.

New Arrival. "MUMMY, MUMMY, LET'S FOLLOW THE CLOWNS."

118   *23 September 1931*

THE OLD-FASHIONED COUPLE GO TO A PYJAMA-PARTY.

119   *23 August 1933*

notice (Plate 113). It seems certain that only a tiny minority wore them, and then mostly in the evening.

The Great War saw a new development in the wearing of trousers. It represented an immeasurable step forward in women's emancipation, for the conscription of all available men to the Front meant that their jobs fell vacant and had to be filled by women, who thereby gained greater economic and social freedom than ever before. The highly vertical silhouette of immediately pre-war fashions had already obliterated many of the differences between men's and women's dress. This, in conjunction with the new demands on women, made it quite easy and natural for them to adopt trousers if they were, for example, working on the land or in a munitions factory (Plate 114). Furthermore, the economic stringencies of the war meant that extravagance in dress came to be seen as unpatriotic and tasteless. Thus we see *Punch*'s land-girls either admitting to a complete lack of women's clothes (Plate 115), or using those they still have to dress a scarecrow (Plate 116).

The 1920s did not see the enthusiastic adoption of trousers for all occasions which might have been expected, and which was often claimed (Plate 117). The post-war mood was one of escapism, and

ANY PORT IN A STORM.

120 *6 September 1933*

women's fashions emulated the childish rather than the manly. Where trousers were worn, it was in the form of garish beach pyjamas, which were sported either at the seaside (Plate 118) or at avant-garde evening parties, at which the unwary might be caught out (Plate 119). The cut of these trousers, which persisted well into the next decade, was anything but practical (Plates 120 and 121), and they were not for general day wear. A newspaper report that two girls were seen walking along Fleet Street in 'gaily-hued beach pyjamas' provoked *Punch*'s derision:

> Blest pair of sirens whose pyjama'd grace
> Enlivened for a brief but welcome space
> The gloomy turmoil of the Street of Ink
> (Though why on earth you did it I can't think),
> Who bore besides the natty slumber-wear,
> It seems, the subtle but distinctive air
> Of having lately photographed St Paul's –
> A thrilling sport, yet scarcely one which calls
> For raiment better suited to the Lido –
> I feel that we who of your exploits read owe
> A debt of thanks 'twere churlish not to pay,

"FURL THE MAINSAIL? NO, NO; FURL HER LADYSHIP'S TROUSERS!"

121 *24 August 1932*

> Not for your valiant but vain essay
> To brighten up the City's sombre streets,
> Nor for your daring photographic feats,
> But for a boon of higher, rarer strain –
> A glimpse of the ineffably inane!

26 August 1931

During the 1930s the passion for outdoor pursuits, and in particular hiking, brought in shorts for leisure wear in a big way, Fougasse reviving Bernard Partridge's joke about the way to Wareham (Plate 122). But it was not until the Second World War that trousers became part of everyday wear, being cheap, warm and practical, qualities epitomized in the siren suit. Wartime women, then, wore trousers almost universally, and those who chose to stay in skirts apparently dwindled to a conspicuous minority (Plate 123), but *Punch* pointed out an absurd anomaly:

> Women wear trousers
> To trail round the shops;
> Women in trousers
> Wield brushes and mops.

" Is this the way to W—A—R—E—H—A—M ?"

122   *19 August 1936*

Women wear trousers
For sleeping and sitting
And pouring out tea in
And doing their knitting.

For cleaning the windows,
And filling the shells,
And taking round letters,
And answering bells.

Women in trousers
(Or leastways in breeches)
Are planting potatoes
And scraping out ditches.

They wear them for punching
Our tickets in trams,
Or pushing their babies
Abroad in their prams,

In fact nearly everything
Under the sun,
But – why *don't* they wear them
For manning a gun?

3 December 194

The return of peace, however, ushered in the romanticism of Dior's New Look. Trousers were firmly established for leisure wear, but post-war woman wanted none of them for either office or evening. She was tired of austerity and practicality and yearned to be seductive again, and post-war man agreed with her. Trousers retained their casual image for another twenty years – in the mid-1960s the magazine *Honey* advised students to make the most of their college years, as this was probably the only time in their lives that they would be able to go to work in trousers. Although trouser suits became high fashion at about this time, many restaurants and clubs, as well as most employers, vetoed them (Plate 24). At the end of the 1960s, when the miniskirt was enjoying its greatest popularity, the story was widely circulated of a girl who was

23   *28 January 1942*

" They're wearing their skirts shorter, I see."

*"Rules are rules. Either **she's** wearing trousers, or **he's** not wearing a tie."*

124   *1 February 1967*

refused admission to Claridge's because she was wearing a trouser suit. With enviable aplomb she removed the trousers and, since the jacket was no shorter than the average skirt, she was allowed in.

Today, the impact of youth fashion and the rise of the women's liberation movement have ensured that trousers are permissible on most occasions. Yet the police force will not contemplate putting their women into them, despite their obvious advantages; many women teachers are still forbidden them; and most people shudder at the thought of nurses in trousers. In the public sector at least, no matter how tough the job, women are still expected to look feminine.

6 Trinity or Girton?

The tendency of one sex to adopt the clothes and appearance of the other is, according to several recent articles in the press, a sure sign of a confused and decadent society. Our own times are, in this respect, likened to pre-war Berlin, where cross-dressing was not uncommon. Where society is confident of its aims, roles tend to be polarized; when there is doubt and questioning, traditional demarcation lines become blurred. At first sight, then, it is rather astonishing to find references to gender confusion as early as the 1840s; but the point here is that in the Victorian age the difference between the sexes was so clear-cut that the slightest overstepping of the line seemed extraordinary. The jokes and allusions exist only because no confusion was possible. Had it been possible, the Victorians would not have made light of it: they would have found it too horrible.

Over the last 150 years, the interchange of dress styles between the sexes has happened in distinct phases. At the beginning of the Victorian age men's and women's clothes were very nearly as different as they could be. It is true that men still padded their chests and nipped in their waists, which gave them a distinctly effeminate look, and it is also true that, before the discovery of aniline dyes, the colours of women's clothes did not present the brilliant contrast to men's that they did later. Nevertheless, women wore soft wool muslins in delicate, blurred prints, while men stuck to plain dark cloth. More importantly, their outlines were totally different. Men were essentially vertical, the trousers fitting closely and smoothly to the leg, the coat long and waisted, and the head topped by a stovepipe hat. Women were pyramidal, their heads closely framed in demure bonnets, their shoulders draped in shawls, and their skirts widening to the ground over a number of petticoats. The air of softness and fragility, the frills and flounces and trimmings, together with the impracticality of this costume, were all considered to express woman's fundamental nature and thus to be – allowing for stylistic

SOMETHING LIKE A BROTHER.

Flora. "THAT'S A VERY PRETTY WAISTCOAT, EMILY !"
Emily. "YES, DEAR. IT BELONGS TO MY BROTHER CHARLES. WHEN HE GOES
OUT OF TOWN HE PUTS ME ON THE FREE LIST, AS HE CALLS IT, OF HIS WARDROBE.
ISN'T IT KIND ?"

" No Collars, Sir ? It must be Miss Julia, for she sent fifteen to wash only last week."

125   *I, 1852, p. 98*   126   *11 December 1858*

variations from one season to the next – immutable. Men and women
led totally different lives, and their clothes expressed this contrast
throughout the Victorian age. In this ethos cross-dressing as a
fashionable device was an impossibility (though as a means to an end it
may have been a necessity, as in the case of Dr 'James' Barry). The
nearest approach to it was that from time to time women would borrow
an item from the male wardrobe, such as the waistcoat (Plate 125) or the
collar (Plate 126), and wear it for a season or two. They were certainly
not motivated by a desire to look like men; much more likely they felt
that their femininity was enhanced by effective contrast. In the 1960s a
wellknown manufacturer of men's clothes circulated advertisements in
which their shirts were worn, very fetchingly, by glamorous and shapely
women. The caption read: 'Looks even better on a man'. A cartoon
parody promptly appeared in which a dour-faced man sported a
woman's foundation garment, with the caption: 'Looks even better on a
woman'; and of course it does not work both ways. Thus in the Victorian
age the borrowing was entirely one-way, and it was not viewed with
favour. If normal 'feminine' clothes provoked amused condescension in
men, the adoption of an alternative was condemned outright. When, at
the end of the 1840s, women sought a more practical form of outdoor
wear than the shawl or lightweight mantle, and lit on the paletot, an
eminently sensible and hard-wearing kind of overcoat, they were

A VERY NATURAL MISTAKE.

Young Lady (who is in Hat and Coat of the period). "CAN I HAVE A MACHINE NOW?"
Bathing Woman. "NOT HERE, SIR!—GENTLEMEN'S BATHING A LITTLE FURTHER DOWN!"

27   *6 September 1856*

severely criticized for poaching on male territory:

> Though there may be one article of male attire that the gentler sex
> will not insist upon the right to wear [Poor *Punch* – scarcely more
> than two years later it was to be further outraged by the
> appearance of bloomers], we perceive a growing disposition
> towards the adoption of other portions of our costume, to an extent
> that has left us no other guide than the bonnet, by which to
> distinguish our male from our female acquaintances. The masculine
> paletot is now so universally adopted for feminine wear, that we are
> in danger of confounding our sons with our daughters, and are
> disposed to confound the arbiters of Fashion who have introduced
> the absurdities of costume that are now so general. We refrain from
> tracing the origin of the nondescript article worn by the ladies of
> the present day; but the antiquarian would tell us that it is a
> modification of the old watchman's coat grafted on the night gown
> of domestic life, with a dash of the primaeval pinafore, and a small
> taste of the antique tippet. We shall be delighted when France
> becomes a little more rational, if it is only for the chance we shall
> then have of seeing the fashions imported thence invested with a
> greater air of rationality.

II, 1849, p. 113

It will be noticed that the alleged irrationality of the paletot consists exclusively in its having been borrowed from the male wardrobe: France is in fact being criticized for being sensible. Be that as it may, the paletot caught on, particularly at the seaside where it was admirably protective against cold winds, and was worn not with a blinkering bonnet but with a jaunty little hat that perched on top of the head and was trimmed either with upstanding feathers or with streamers. *Punch* would have us believe that young women thus attired were mistaken for men by bathing-machine attendants (Plate 127), and that young men were forced to find alternatives to their usurped coats and hats (Plate 128), while aunts vented their sarcasm on their nieces' unfeminine attire (Plate 129). Obviously this alleged confusion was a complete fiction, but it must have been a powerful one, since it formed the subject of a joke even in the heyday of the crinoline (Plate 130), at a time when the steel cage separated the men from the girls more conspicuously than ever before. The short jacket of the 1860s gave way to the full-length Ulster of the 1870s which, when worn with a plain round hat, once again provoked a rash of jokes (Plates 131 and 132). It is true that both hair

128 *13 October 1855*   129 *4 July 1868*

Charles. " FIGURE, INDEED ! WHAT'S A FELLOW TO DO ? A MAN MUST WEAR SOMETHING. HATS AND COATS ARE OUT OF THE QUESTION—THEY ARE REALLY SO VERY EFFEMINATE."

EVIDENT.

Emma. " WELL, AUNTY, HOW DO YOU THINK THE SEASIDE AGREES WITH ME ?"
Aunty. " LOR', MY LOVE, IT'S MADE QUITE A MAN OF YOU ?"

and skirts were effectively concealed by this costume, but the absurdity
of the claim that women could therefore be mistaken for men is exposed
in Plate 133. For the shop-girl who is enthusing over the manliness of the
coat she is modelling is unmistakably female: even in an enveloping
overcoat, a woman's figure, when corseted to small-waisted perfection
and supplemented by a bustle, is not to be confused with a man's.

By the last quarter of the century, the demand for women's
emancipation had gathered considerable momentum. New ground had
been broken and more was being pressed for, with the result that, while
some women were restless and frustrated at the amount still to be
gained, others were confused and frightened by what had already been
achieved, and uncertain of what they really wanted. With women
militant or bewildered and men threatened, there came to be a feeling of
confusion over the traditional roles of the sexes (Plate 134). In his book
The Dark Angel Fraser Harrison has suggested that this confusion
reached its most vivid expression in George du Maurier's best-selling
novel *Trilby* (1894). The hero, Harrison points out, is

30   *1 March 1862*

HARRY TAKES HIS COUSINS TO SEE THE HOUNDS MEET.

Enter MAMMA AND AUNT ELLEN.

Mamma (*to Old Woman*). "PRAY, HAVE YOU MET TWO LADIES AND A GENTLEMAN?"

Old Woman. "WELL, I MET THREE PEOPLE—BUT, LA! THERE, I CAN'T TELL LADIES FROM GENTLEMEN NOW-A-DAYS—WHEN *I* WAS A GAL, &C. &C."

LEVELLING TENDENCY OF MODERN DRESS.

Old Gentleman (shocked beyond description) to Verger. "DON'T YOU THINK THOSE YOUTHS HAD BETTER BE TOLD TO TAKE THEIR HATS OFF?"

Verger. "TAKE THEIR 'ATS OFF! BLESS YOU, SIR, THOSE ARE THE *DEAN'S* YOUNG LADIES!"

131 *17 March 1877*   132 *24 November 1877*

VERY NATURAL.

Mrs. Broadrib (sternly). "ARE YOU AWARE, SIR, THAT THIS IS THE LADIES' WAITING-ROOM!!"

(Mistaking Angelica Stodge, in her "Ulster" and round hat, on her way home from South Kensington, for one of the ruder Sex!!")

THE NE PLUS ULSTER.

Fair Customer. "BUT IT MAKES ONE LOOK SO LIKE A MAN!"
Showwoman. "THAT'S JUST THE BEAUTY OF IT, MISS!"

133   *11 December 1880*

134   *10 April 1880*

"MAN OR WOMAN?"—A TOSS UP.

"DRESSES ARE STILL UNIVERSALLY CUT EN CŒUR. A VERY DRESSY TOILETTE, AND ONE, MUCH WORN NOW, FOR THE EVENING, IS OF BLACK BROCHÉ OR CLOTH MATERIAL CUT EN HABIT D'HOMME, WITH PLAIN OR KILTED SKIRT, VERY TIGHT; FOR FAIR LADIES IT IS VERY BECOMING TO OMIT A TUCKER, AND HAVE THE BLACK WITH NO SOFTENING."
Journal des Modes, 1st April.

. . . small, slender, graceful, and well-built, his forehead is straight, white, and blue-veined, his eyes are large and dark blue, his hair is coal-black, and his hands and feet are very small. The inattentive reader may be forgiven at this point for imagining that he has just read a description of the heroine, so closely does Little Billee's appearance tally with the conventions of Victorian beauty.

The heroine, on the other hand, is extremely tall, with a loud voice, a massive chin and large feet, and she makes her first appearance dressed in a soldier's greatcoat. Considering the book's phenomenal popularity, Harrison thinks it 'reasonable to suggest that the characteristics with which Trilby has been endowed presumably represented a kind of sexuality that was in accord with public taste. And yet, du Maurier had created a beau ideal whose sexual charisma chiefly lay in her boyishness, and occasionally even in her manliness'.

Borrowings from the male wardrobe became more consistent. The enthusiasm for sport demanded a less constricting costume than the rigid bodices and elaborate skirts of the late 1870s and 1880s, and women turned naturally to men's clothes for inspiration (Plate 135). It was neither easy nor safe to ride a bicycle in a long skirt, so cycling knickerbockers were introduced. Like the bloomers of forty years earlier, their only claim to manliness was that they were bifurcated; but this, together with the aura of fastness and independence which surrounded the sport, was enough to make du Maurier revive one of his own jokes of twenty years before, exchanging Ulsters and round hats for knickerbockers and boaters (Plate 136). Meanwhile the masculinization of women's costume was receiving a further impetus from the feminist quarter. Despising the frills and fripperies of fashionable women as symbols of enslavement, the 'Modern Woman' adopted a serge tailor-made with a high stiff collar and tie, hoping thus to prove herself beyond question man's equal, but in fact merely exchanging one set of uncomfortable garments for another (Plate 137). *Punch* bewailed the trend:

> Kitty's birthday's to-morrow; say, what shall I get her?
>   A diamond heart, or a locket of pearls?
> Or think you a necklace or belt would be better?
>   Or tortoiseshell combs for her dear little curls?
> A brooch for her throat, or a ring for her finger?
>   A boa or a tippet? New kerchiefs or hose?
> A desk, where the scents of the Orient linger?
>   At trifles like these she would turn up her nose.
>
> For KITTY this winter would have you believe her
>   The like of her possible master and lord.
> A cabby or coachman would covet her beaver,
>   Her collars and shirt-fronts are stiff as a board.
> Her dresses are cut by a tailor of fashion,
>   Her jackets are homespun, her coats are of frieze,
> For knick-knacks men love she's developed a passion
>   That almost amounts to a kind of disease.
>
> Away then to Bond Street, for clear is my mission.
>   I'll buy her a cane, or a glass for her eye,
> Some links, of the kind that are known as 'perdition',
>   A hundred cigars, or a masculine tie.
> For KITTY's a man, and you must not forget it,
>   But sometimes I wish, though I dare not complain,
> That Fashion, most captious of tyrants, would let it
>   Be *chic* for our girls to be women again.

18 October 1905

THE STERNER SEX!

"Hullo, Gerty! You've got Fred's Hat on, and his Cover Coat?"

"Yes. Don't you like it?"

"Well — it makes you look like a Young Man, you know, and that's so Effeminate!"

135 *26 September 1891*

136 *13 June 1896*

RATIONAL COSTUME.

The Vicar of St. Winifred-in-the-Wold (to fair Bicyclists). "It is customary for Men, I will not say *Gentlemen*, to remove their Hats on entering a Church!"

Confusion of the Ladies Rota and Ixiona Bykewell.

REGRETTABLE SET-BACK TO THE "ENTENTE."

French Visitor at Exhibition (reciting verbatim from his phrase-book). "'Sir, or Madam, as the case may be.'" . . . .

137   *1 July 1908*

THE SEX QUESTION.
(A STUDY IN BOND STREET.)

138   *5 April 1911*

So far any *rapprochement* in the dress of the sexes had been a question of women borrowing, at first sporadically and then more consistently, from men. A few artistic pioneers had perceived that men's dress would be immeasurably improved if it could only do a little borrowing itself, particularly in the areas of texture and colour. In 1882 Oscar Wilde observed that 'perhaps one of the most difficult things for us to do is to choose a notable and joyous dress for men. There would be more joy in life if we were to accustom ourselves to use all the beautiful colours we can in fashioning our own clothes'. But his own efforts in this field met largely with derision. The average Victorian man sought merely to be inconspicuous: an active interest in clothes would have been an admission of frivolity, or worse.

In the second decade of this century two factors, not directly connected with women's emancipation, brought men's and women's dress closer together. The new vertical look for women, heralded by *Punch* in 1909 (see Chapter 2), meant that for the first time in a hundred years men and women shared an approximate outline (Plate 138). Corsets lengthened, waists expanded while hips dwindled, and there was an increase in plain, ready-to-wear coats and skirts, so that well before war broke out women were prepared for the masculine role they would be playing. And the war's effect, of propelling women into all sorts of men's jobs on the land and in workshops, meant that a woman in

First Officer (in spasm of jealousy). "WHO'S THE KNOCK-KNEED CHAP WITH YOUR SISTER, OLD MAN?"
Second Officer. "MY OTHER SISTER."

139   *29 May 1918*

trousers was not seen either as a hussy or as a rabid feminist, but simply as a patriot (Plate 139).

The women of the 1920s were naturally determined to consolidate their recent victories in the field of emancipation. They did this not by the indiscriminate wearing of trousers which many people had foretold – trousers were kept for sport and evening wear – but, infinitely more dramatically, by cutting their hair. Anita Loos, the author of *Gentlemen Prefer Blondes*, claims to have been a pioneer in this field. In *A Girl Like I*, an autobiography from which she has artfully expunged all dates, she describes accompanying D.W. Griffith to New York to promote his film *Intolerance*, for which she had written the subtitles (which places the incident some time in 1916):

> On reaching a suite at the Algonquin, I immediately set about doing something I'd had in mind for years. . . . With hands actually trembling in excitement, I proceeded to whack off my hair, becoming one of the very first girls of our century ever to be 'bobbed'.

Any change in a girl's hair-do produces a psychological effect which it must be difficult for men to understand. Just as Samson lost strength by getting his hair bobbed, girls gain theirs through the process, a fact which must also have been discovered by Joan of

PARDONABLE MISTAKE ON THE PART OF AN ABSENT-
MINDED HAIRDRESSER.

Arc and . . . George Sand. . . . Sitting in the parlor of that
Algonquin suite, my feet missing the floor by a good sixteen inches, I
held my shorn head high and proceeded to give forth on D.W.
Griffith, *Intolerance*, and culture in general.

For centuries hair had been woman's crowning glory, cascading in
luxurious ringlets or heaped in elaborate coils, the supreme symbol of
her womanhood, whence St Paul's decree that it should be covered up.
Even in the days of the Regency, when it had been worn short, it had
curled coquettishly over the neck and forehead. The uncompromising
severity of the shingle or the Eton crop, with the accompanying shaved
neck, was something quite new (Plate 140), and most men hated it.

'My dear girl,' Michael had said, when shingling came in, 'to
please me, don't! Your *nuque* will be too bristly for kisses.'
'My dear boy,' she had answered, 'as if one could help it!
You're always the same with any new fashion!'

John Galsworthy, *The Silver Spoon*

But despite male protests, short hair became universal, for it felt
modern and functional, the antithesis to Victorian sentimentality, and it

hort-sighted Old Lady (at boarding-house). "EXCUSE ME—DID YOU SAY YOU WERE GOING UP TO TRINITY OR GIRTON NEXT TERM?"

41   *16 September 1925*

142   *21 March 1928*

Young Woman (looking at photograph of friend's fiancé). "WELL, GOD BLESS YOU, MY DEAR, CONGRATULATIONS AND ALL THAT. E CERTAINLY LOOKS TWICE THE MAN YOU ARE."

Diehard (stroking his beard). "MY DEAR GIRL, IT'S OUR ONLY CHANCE LEFT. AS SOON AS YOU CAN IMITATE THIS WE'RE DONE."

143 *11 February 1925*

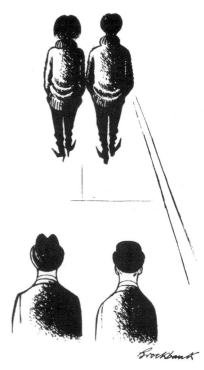

"*The American Army has got radar that can detect the difference between a man and a woman a mile away.*"

144 *26 July 1961*

went with the drinking and smoking which had also been appropriated from the men. Thus, although women's clothes in the 1920s were not predominantly masculine, their hair-styles and their demeanour were and young women – academics perhaps – with a taste for severity in dress might end up looking very manly indeed (Plates 141 and 142).

By 1925 the widespread fashion for such 'unisex' garments as knitted Fair Isle jerseys and stockings led *Punch* to the somewhat exaggerated claim that facial hair was the only sure way of telling a man from a woman (Plate 143). Six years later, when the pendulum of fashion had swung once again towards contrast, Eric Gill argued in his provocative little book *Clothes* that no further differentiation was needed. Several decades ahead of his time, Gill suggested that 'the present divorce between men and women, so graphically displayed in the violent contrast between their clothes, might be healed as well by women adopting men's clothes as by men adopting women's'. The emancipated look of the 1920s had by now fallen from favour and given way to the more traditionally feminine look of the 1930s, with softer hairstyles and longer skirts, and a slender but curvaceous figure, all in marked contrast to man's stolid monochrome. Gill recognized that 'many otherwise sane people will go almost mad' at his proposed *rapprochement*, but pointed out that nature could be trusted to prevent actual confusion.

> It is natural to dress up; it is natural to wear clothes. Both men and women have bodies and two arms and two legs. Both walk and both run. Both work and both play. But universally, apart from special circumstances wherein hiding seems desirable, all men and all women expose the face, and the face of woman remains hairless, but man grows a beard – and the beard grows at the very moment when differentiation becomes imperative. How simple, how excellent, how supremely intelligent!

By the outbreak of the Second World War women had discovered that to do a man's job in a man's world it was not necessary for a woman to look like a man. Consequently, although nearly all women went into trousers or a male-inspired uniform, there was a strong emphasis on hair-styles and make-up which were considered 'glamorous'. With the return of peace, and relatively normal social life, the mood, despite desperate austerity, was of *vive la différence*. Women, and men too, were sick of skimpy, unflattering clothes, and the New Look caught on, despite government disapproval, because it expressed women's longing for a conventional romantic role.

The sexes remained polarized in conventional circles, but during the 1950s a new style of dress emerged among students and beatniks, which consisted of longer hair for men, and tight jeans and shapeless black sweaters for both sexes (Plate 144). The originality of this get-up lay in the fact that it represented not a desire by women to claim male privileges via their costume, but a wish by both sexes to cast off social restrictions and all the paraphernalia of worldliness and snobbishness with which fashionable dress was encrusted. This trend continued with modifications only of degree until the 1960s, when from being merely shaggy men's hair became truly long. Now for the first time there was a genuine possibility of the sexes being confused with one another (Plate 145). For this was the first time that men had poached on traditionally female territory. While all the borrowing and copying was done by women, with men staying entrenched in their traditionally masculine role, the difference between the sexes remained all too apparent. But with genuine interchange the question became more complex. Towards the end of the 1960s unisex was launched as the fashion of the day, capitalizing on both the existing trend of clothes-sharing – the abolition

"Same old story—boy meets girl but doesn't know it."

145   *6 April 1966*

of the female figure meant that girls could wear men's shirts and trousers – and the functionalism of many 1960s clothes. But unisex enjoyed only a brief innings, precisely because it was so unexciting. Despite the fact that romantic frilled shirts and velvet trousers had been as much a part of 1960s menswear as practical denims, it offered no scope for men to dress in a feminine way (Plate 146). That was left to Mick Jagger, who appeared at the July 1969 Hyde Park concert in a white minidress. (The *News of the World* described it the following day, with admirable restraint, as being 'cool and summery'.) Pop stars can act with greater bravado than ordinary people, it is undeniable that they are trend-setters, and it was through their influence that androgyny became an increasingly fashionable look in the 1970s. Few young men went as far as David Bowie in his Ziggy Stardust persona, but they did wear make-up, which only a few years before would have been unthinkable (Plate 147), and there was a pronounced ambiguity about their sartorial models. One mother at this time snapped at her fifteen-year-old son to remove his blue eye-shadow, 'You look just like Marlene Dietrich', only to be rapturously thanked for such a flattering comparison.

Today we have the deliberately disturbing confusion of such characters as Boy George and Grace Jones. It is still confusion rather than deception, but it seems to say that whatever the differences may be between women and men, they are not to be defined in terms of dress.

"*The lads at the works are saying you've got the wrong idea about unisex clothes.*"

146   *23 July 1969*

147   *10 October 1973*

"*I don't care if all the other boys do it— you're not using my eye make up.*"

7 Seaside Costumes

Ever since the beneficial effects of salt water were first propounded, and
Scarborough advertised itself as a bathing resort, soon after 1730, the
British have loved seaside holidays. The early Victorian age saw
the full flowering of this tradition. The overcrowding, the pollution and
the unwholesomeness of the big industrial cities made a fortnight's fresh
air by the sea seem irresistibly attractive, and the advent of cheap and
efficient railway travel placed such a luxury well within the reach of the
lower middle class as well as their social superiors. And for those who
could not afford so long a stay, there were plenty of day excursions.
Ruskin's famous dictum that, thanks to the railways, 'every fool in
Buxton can be at Bakewell in half-an-hour, and every fool in Bakewell at
Buxton', was nowhere more true than in the resorts which sprang up all
around Britain's coast from Blackpool to Scarborough. July and August
saw a large-scale exodus from the cities, acknowledged and exploited
not only by the resorts themselves, where lodgings were exorbitantly
priced and landladies tyrannical, but by the publishers of innumerable
novels 'for seaside reading', and the designers of special seaside fashions.

The Victorians' idea of a seaside holiday was very different from
ours. Not for them the hours of prostrate sunbathing, interrupted only
by forays into the water. They neither sought the sun nor, in the English
climate, could have been sure of finding it anyway, and bathing was still
viewed as a penance, an unpleasant if wholesome ritual to be performed
as early in the day as possible. For the rest of the time, while the lower
classes indulged unselfconsciously in food, drink and the varied
entertainments of the sea-front, those with a claim to gentility wandered
endlessly between the library, the assembly rooms and the promenade,
seeing and being seen. At Ramsgate, the up-market resort where
Dickens's Tuggs family spent their holiday,

> . . . it was a fine, bright, clear day, with a light breeze from the
> sea. . . . The ladies were employed in needlework, or watch-guard

EXTRACT FROM "THE FASHIONS."

Our Autumn Costumes suitable for the Country and Sea-side are now Ready."

148   *30 October 1869*

49   *2 September 1871*

150   *II, 1855, p. 142*

SIGNS OF THE BATHING SEASON.

" How is this, Mr. Tongs? You have not sent Home my Travelling Chignon, yet?"

" Beg Pardon, M'm, I'm sure. But the Fact is, we've been so Busy Makin' up our Seaside Back 'Air.''

TERRIBLE ACCIDENT.

" We knew how it would be—Girls holding those great Round Hats over their Eyes so that they can't see where they are going.—Why, here's Flora Plumley run right into the arms of *that* young Horace Spanker, who hasn't a penny."—*Extract from our Aunt's Letter.*

THE SEA-SIDE HAT.
WHAT IS ENOUGH FOR ONE IS ENOUGH FOR TWO.

151 *II, 1854, p. 122*
152 *19 August 1876*

SEA-SIDE COSTUMES.
A DISTINCTION WITH A DIFFERENCE. THE GENTLEMEN HAVE TWO LEGS TO
THEIR TROUSERS : THE LADIES ONLY *ONE*.

making, or knitting, or reading novels; the gentlemen were reading newspapers and magazines; the children were digging holes in the sand with wooden spades, and collecting water therein; the nursemaids, with their youngest charges in their arms, were running in after the waves, and then running back with the waves after them; and, now and then, a little sailing-boat either departed with a gay and talkative cargo of passengers, or returned with a very silent and particularly uncomfortable-looking one.

Later in the day,

. . . the library was crowded. There were the same ladies, and the same gentlemen, who had been on the sands in the morning, and on the pier the day before. There were young ladies, in maroon-coloured gowns and black velvet bracelets, dispensing fancy articles in the shop, and presiding over games of chance in the concert-room. There were marriageable daughters, and marriage-making mammas, gaming and promenading, and turning over music, and flirting. There were some male beaux doing the sentimental in whispers, and others doing the ferocious in moustache. There were Mrs Tuggs in amber, Miss Tuggs in sky-blue, Mrs Captain Waters in pink.

LES MATELOTS.

53   *26 August 1931*

Romance was one of the chief preoccupations of the seaside
holiday, and it was fostered by the informality of the surroundings.
Away from everyday cares and duties, the strict code of Victorian
behaviour could be slightly relaxed. Moreover, it was difficult to place
people socially with perfect precision when meeting them on neutral
ground. That this anonymity could be used for fraudulent purposes is
the upshot of the Tuggs's story, but it could also lend spice and a touch of
mystery to a romantic encounter. Thus it is that the seaside costumes so
widely advertised in the fashion magazines were designed entirely with a
view to attracting the opposite sex, and with never a thought for the
realities of salt water, sand and wind (Plate 148). At the beach, and there
only, young mid-Victorian women were allowed to let their hair flow
freely over their shoulders for the admiration of passing young men.
Luxuriant 'back hair' was such a desirable feature that a brisk trade was
carried on in false switches (Plate 149). The jokes about seaside costumes
in the 1840s and 1850s mostly have romantic themes, and show how
such fashions as the round hats designed to ward off the sun could be
adapted for other, more interesting purposes (Plates 150 and 151). But
the easy-going holiday atmosphere of the resorts also meant that they
could act as a testing-ground for new ideas in dress. It was at the beach
that women first adopted the windproof 'paletot' jackets which later
found their way into city fashion (see Chapter 6). And there in the mid-

"*Chicken!*"

154   *1 July 1964*

1860s that skirts were introduced which could be hitched up by means of
strings, and in the 1870s that women's costume edged closer to men's
(Plate 152). Nearer to our own time, in the 1920s, it was on the beach
that young women first wore trousers with impunity (Plate 153), and
there in the 1960s that the topless fashion came into its own (Plate 154).

Swimming-costumes were seldom illustrated, since they were
glimpsed rather than seen. The usual procedure was to change inside a
bathing-machine, have a quick dip in the water behind it, and then get
back in and put on ordinary clothes again. The Tuggs family, unversed
in the ways of the seaside, viewed the whole process with alarm:

'Why, I'm blest if there ain't some ladies a-going in!' exclaimed Mr
Joseph Tuggs, with intense astonishment. . . . And, sure enough,
four young ladies, each furnished with a towel, tripped up the steps
of a bathing machine. In went the horse, floundering about in the
water; round turned the machine; down sat the driver; and
presently out burst the young ladies aforesaid, with four distinct
splashes. . . .

'Why, here's some gentlemen a-going in on this side,'
exclaimed Mrs Tuggs, in a tone of horror.

Three machines – three horses – three flounderings – three
turnings round – three splashes – three gentlemen disporting
themselves in the water like so many dolphins.

Women's swimming-costumes, which were very similar to bloomers, consisted of a loose, belted tunic with sleeves, worn over full trousers of varying length. The outfit was completed by canvas shoes and a mob-cap. The costumes were usually made of navy blue serge or flannel, but, however voluminous and modest when first put on, they clung tightly to the figure when wet, so that one of Dickens's swimmers 'looked as if she was enveloped in a patent mackintosh of scanty dimensions'. At the beginning of the Victorian period, the daily swim consisted of the briefest possible immersion, but during the 1860s women began to be interested in swimming as a form of exercise and as a useful accomplishment in case of accident. This interest was reflected in a regular swimming column in the magazine *The Queen*, by a correspondent signing himself 'Un Giovonotto', but it did not result in any significant change in costume design. Indeed Giovonotto's researches did not lead him to advocate any change. Wishing to establish whether women were capable of swimming in their everyday clothes (assuming, for example, that they had fallen out of a boat), the brave man made the

155   *4 September 1897*

ALTOGETHER SATISFACTORY.

Aunt Fanny. "I DO LIKE THESE FRENCH WATERING-PLACES. THE BATHING COSTUME IS SO SENSIBLE!"
Hilda. "OH, YES, AUNTIE! AND SO BECOMING!"

["Bathing-dresses are more elaborate than ever this year."—Vide *Ladies' Papers*.]

Amy. "Well, I suppose we may as well be going into the sea—come along, Maud."
Maud. "My dear Amy, what *are* you talking about? Why! it would absolutely *ruin* my dress!"

experiment himself, donning a pink spotted dress for the purpose, and enduring the astonished stares of the crowd which quickly gathered to watch him. He found that, with the exception of the wire crinoline, women's clothes, and more particularly their full skirts, actually helped him to stay afloat. (The crinoline turned him head over heels in the water.)

Men generally bathed in the nude, through trunks were occasionally worn from the beginning of the century. In the last quarter they became more common, though they seem to have been a matter for local provision rather than items of personal dress. The Revd Francis Kilvert, visiting the Isle of Wight in 1874, wrote indignantly:

At Shanklin one has to adopt the detestable custom of bathing in drawers. If ladies don't like to see men naked why don't they keep away from the sight? To-day I had a pair of drawers given me which I could not keep on. The rough waves stripped them off and tore them down round my ancles [*sic*]. While thus fettered I was seized and flung down by a heavy sea which retreating suddenly left me lying naked on the sharp shingle from which I rose streaming with blood. After this I took the wretched and dangerous rag off and of course there were some ladies looking on as I came up out of the water.

Shopman (discussing bathing costume). "REALLY, I CAN'T UNDERSTAND IT SHRINKING. UNLESS—ER—YOU'VE ACTUALLY BEEN IN THE SEA WITH IT."

57   *22 July 1931*

Children also bathed with nothing on, and the sight of a naked little girl sitting on the sands looking out to sea aroused Kilvert to one of his most purple passages. But women encountering such sights averted their eyes, as Gwen Raverat remembered:

> All summer, Sheep's Green and Coe Fen were pink with boys, as naked as God made them; for bathing drawers did not exist then; or, at least, not on Sheep's Green. You could see the pinkness, dancing about, quite plain, from the end of our Big Island. Now to go Up the River, the goal of all the best picnics, the boats had to go right by the bathing places, which lay on both sides of the narrow stream. These dangerous straits were taken in silence, and at full speed. The Gentlemen were set to the oars – in this context one obviously thinks of them as Gentlemen – and each Lady unfurled a parasol, and, like an ostrich, buried her head in it, and gazed earnestly into its silky depths, until the crisis was past, and the river was decent again.

As more and more people went abroad for their holidays, the arrangements on the beaches at home began to be unfavourably

compared with those on the Continent, and the bathing-machine fell
from favour. In 1871 a writer in *The Graphic* pointed out that it was
absurd 'to employ a man, a horse and a great house on wheels to enable a
British human creature to dip himself in the sea', and soon afterwards
the machines were superseded by stationary huts at the top of the beach.
It was now necessary to make the journey from hut to water's edge in
one's costume and in full public view, and the bathing-dress rapidly
reached the degree of elaboration which already prevailed in France
(Plate 155). Fashion overcame function, and the prime purpose of the
costume was obscured and even impeded (Plate 156). A description in
the daily press of an inexpensive *toilette* for the beach prompted *Punch* to a
poem, 'On Delia - Going to Bathe':

> When the sun is warm and high,
>   When no zephyr blows
> Rudely from a tumbled sky,
>   And my lady Delia goes
> Down to brave the limpid sea,
> Passing fair, I ween, is she.
>
> You shall find her slender shape
>   Pleasingly displayed
> In a garb of costly crepe –
>   Finest cloth and latest shade –
> With, perchance, the happy grace
> Of some ancient Irish lace.
>
> Over this a chiffon wrap
>   Flows in various curves;
> While upon her head a cap
>   (Nothing less than satin) serves
> To protect her from the day
> And the too-insistent spray.
>
> Thus, in part, is Delia clad,
>   Yet not thus alone;
> Corsets for her figure add
>   Something that remains their own;
> What it is one may not tell,
> But they seem to do it well.

"I WANT A BATHING-COSTUME. I DON'T MIND WHAT COLOUR, BUT, PLEASE—*(shudder)*—LET IT BE A WARM ONE."

Aunt Jane. "REALLY, GLADYS, THE BATHING DRESSES YOU GIRLS WEAR ARE DISGRACEFUL. LOOK AT ME; DO *I* SHOW MY FIGURE?"

Yes, but these were not enow.
   Pardon if I beg
That, for once, you would allow
   Mention of a maiden's leg.
('Legs' were better – she has two –
But, in verses, one will do)

What, then, is my Delia's whim
   With regard to these?
Silken stockings, neat and trim,
Rich and radiant – never limb
Looked so vivid and so slim –
   Muse, be steady, if you please;
Coldly let us add, my Muse,
Reference to her satin shoes.

Thus equipped in every sort,
   When the weather's fine,
Forth my Delia goes to sport
   By the gay and sparkling brine.
*　*　*　*　*　*　*　*　*　*　*
At the least approach of rain
In my Delia goes again.

14 August 1912

First Critic (in simple bathing-dress, remarking on elaborate costume of lady in foreground). "I CALL IT MOST UNPATRIOTIC."
Second Critic. "YES, WORSE THAN THAT—IT'S BAD FORM."

160   *5 July 1916*   161   *12 August 1925*

MANNERS AND MODES.

Lady of Fashion. "HEAVENS! IT'S TOO STUFFY TO-DAY FOR A BATHING-COSTUME. I MUST GET INTO MY ORDINARY THINGS."

It is amusing to note that while swimsuits of recent times have been more functional in appearance than the outfit described above, the notion that their prime purpose is for display rather than immersion has persisted, to witness the stern injunction on some bikini labels to 'Dry Clean Only', and the little scene in Plate 157. Although swimming had by now lost most of its medicinal connotations, many people still entered the water reluctantly and out of a sense of duty, rather than for any real enjoyment (Plate 158).

In the years immediately preceding the Great War, swimming-costumes became streamlined and figure-hugging, to the disgust of the older generation (Plate 159), though during the war itself their economical lines and lack of ornament conformed to the rule of austerity (Plate 160). With the return of peace, however, elaborate confections reappeared which were better suited to the boudoir than the beach (Plate 161). During this period modesty was preserved first by the introduction of dressing-bags, which afforded a measure of privacy while changing (Plate 162), and second by the regulation enforced on

62 *13 September 1911*

THE DRESSING-BAG HALF-STEP, AS DANCED IN THE CORNISH RIVIERA.

Lady (coming from the sea). "Oh! excuse me—you probably don't know, as you've only just arrived—but, accordin[g] to the regulations of this silly place, you mustn't walk across the beach without a garment that covers you fro[m] head to foot."

163   *28 August 1912*

many beaches that bathers should cover themselves completely wher[e] not actually in the water (Plate 163). At this time, of course, nobod[y] would have dreamt of wearing bathing-costumes anywhere else but o[n] the beach itself, so it is amusing to see that twenty years later th[e] prohibition had been extended to the streets, and that even then it wa[s] proving difficult to implement (Plate 164).

The cult of fitness and health in the 1930s meant that all sports including swimming, were taken seriously. Swimming-costumes shed their frills and fuss and assumed clean functional lines. Their size wa[s] also reduced more than ever before, and the two-piece made its firs[t] appearance (Plate 165). As the cult of the tan developed in the ensuing decades it became everyone's aim to expose more and more o[f] themselves to the rays of the sun, and the fairly solid two-piece of th[e] 1930s dwindled gradually into the exiguous bikinis of the past tw[o] decades or so (Plate 166), until, on the (mostly continental) 'topless' beaches, all that is required is a minute triangle of cloth.

In the Victorian age suntans were considered vulgar, a sign o[f] physical labour performed in the open air, and everybody took steps t[o] avoid them. Sun-bonnets were worn, parasols and sunshades wer[e] carried, and as a last resort Rowland's Kalydor could be applied as [a] kind of bleach. Seaside fashions were distinguished by broad-brimme[d] hats (as already shown in Plates 150 and 151), and a feature of the lat[e]

"EMBARRASSMENT OF SEASIDE POLICEMAN WHO HAS RECEIVED STRICT ORDERS TO SUMMON ANY INDIVIDUAL WALKING IN THE STREET WEARING BATHING-DRESS WITHOUT A WRAP."

64　*27 July 1932*

"I'M SURE YOUR MOTHER WOULD BE SHOCKED IF SHE SAW YOU IN THAT BATHING-COSTUME."
"I'M SURE SHE WOULD—IT'S HERS."

165　*8 August 1934*

"Dear Mr. Punch,
  "I can bear it no longer—I say they have no business to wear them. Why they make their dear beautiful heads look like cowls on chimney-pots, or the hoods of bathing-machines; or, what is worse, they suggest the idea of sore eyes—and all for what? to save their complexions, forsooth—stuff! Pray, dear Punch, put them down—or rather, put them up—or rather, destroy them altogether. You will see what I allude to from the accompanying sketch, done by our friend—you know who—
  "Yours, a most extraordinary and enthusiastic admirer of lovely woman,
  "The Buoy at the Nore."

*"Second floor for dress ties,
   sir. These are bikinis."*

166   *8 January 1969*

167   *II, 1848, p. 134*

1840s was a kind of collapsible hood stretched over cane hoops which could be pulled right over the face to shade it from the sun. As they also protected the wearers from passing glances, these hoods were highly unpopular with the male sex, and were promptly dubbed 'uglies' (Plate 167). As women became more active towards the end of the century, they found it harder to protect themselves from the effect of the sun. Clothes for the beach were considerably less revealing than evening dress at this time, which could lead to unfortunate results (Plate 168). By the 1920s, however, a profound change in attitudes had been effected, and now a healthy bronzed look was *de rigueur* to accompany the new slim, taut figure and general air of athletic prowess. If the required degree of tan could not be accomplished by natural means (Plate 169), it was always possible to invoke artificial ones (Plate 170).

But while most people threw themselves enthusiastically into sun-worshipping, others could not overcome their self-consciousness in the face of all this nudity (Plate 171), and a few were revolted by it:

At Peauville by the Norman coast,
  Ere summer's best had gone,
I saw them lying out to roast
  With nearly nothing on.

WFUL EFFECT OF TOO MUCH LAWN-TENNIS BY THE SEA!

"Don't worry, Darling, you'll look quite respectable in a day or two."

First Lady. "WHO'S THE DAGO?"
Second Lady. "MY DEAR! OH, OF COURSE YOU DON'T REMEMBER. IT'S MY HUSBAND. HE'S HAD TOO MUCH ARTIFICIAL SUNLIGHT."

170   *4 January 1928*   171   *21 August 1935*

"YE KNOW, ADMIRAL, I'M SURE IT'S VERY HEALTHY AND ALL THAT, BUT IN THIS SUNBATHING KIT I FEEL—AH—A CERTAIN LOSS OF *PRESTIGE*."

Their aspect in the simmering heat
   Recalled an uncooked chop;
I never saw so much raw meat
   Outside a butcher's shop.

Along the pebbly plage they stretched,
   Between the wooden groynes,
In just a brassiere, lightly sketched,
   And slips for their sirloins.

Full length they lay on front and back
   Trying with all their might
To tan their bodies brown or black;
   It was a nauseous sight.

As followers of the negroid art
   That governs modern whims
They thus exposed the major part
   Of their unlovely limbs.

I saw the platinum blonde intent
   To be a skin-brunette;
While those with natural swarth were bent
   On growing swarthier yet.

And when one side began to burn
   They greased it to and fro,
And turned it round like chefs that turn
   A steak or tournedos.

I found my appetite displaced
   By thoughts of tribal meals,
Of savage men to whom the taste
   Of human flesh appeals.

And I remarked with bitter mirth,
   'Pray Heaven, I never shall
In any future life on earth
   Be born a cannibal.'

Then from those forms that vexed the bile
   My stomach sought relief
In visions of my native isle,
   The home of well-roast beef.

I pictured, sharing my repast,
   Beauty unspoilt – her face,
Neck, arms and legs (assumed, these last)
   White as the lily's grace;

Touched with the bloom that tints the peach,
   But nothing red or crude
To make me think of Peauville's beach
   And put me off my food.

21 September 1932

8   Protest Clothes

SEA-SIDE TOILETTE. This striking picturesque toilette consists of a princesse dress of mandarin yellow silk, over which is worn a sleeveless polonaise of ivory white India cashmere. The skirt of the dress is simply trimmed with a closely gathered flounce, surmounted by a reversed heading, and supported by a *balayeuse* of white muslin, edged with Valenciennes. The polonaise, which is very clinging, and falls gracefully over the train, is bordered with black velvet ribbon, embroidered with shaded green, yellow ochre, and Egyptian red arabesques. The sleeves of the dress have black velvet cuffs, trimmed in a similar manner. The polonaise is laced in front with a white silk cord, and is drawn in around the hips by a heavy mandarin yellow cord and tassels. Both the dress waist and polonaise open low at the throat, and are furnished with a double turned-down collar, one of yellow silk and the other of white cashmere, under which a broad mandarin yellow ribbon is passed, and tied carelessly in a bow in front. White rice straw hat, with a high square crown and turned-up brim, under which is a wreath of shaded yellow roses. A *panache* of white feathers covers the crown in front, while a large white plume falls on the nape of the neck. A large rosette of mandarin yellow ribbon completes the trimming. Mandarin yellow parasol, lined with white, and finished on top with a cluster of yellow flowers.

Harper's Bazaar, 11 August 1877

It was against mainstream fashion like this that a dress of protest was first conceived.

The dress of protest is not to be confused with dress reform, though the two have certain elements in common. Neither can exist where fashion is the preserve of a few rich people: if it is a minority interest there can be no urgent need to reform it, and no satisfaction to be gained by

FAINT PRAISE.

Æsthetic Lady. "Is not that Mrs. Brabazon, whose Photograph is in all the Shop Windows?"
The Professor. "It is. She is Handsome, is she not?"
Æsthetic Lady. "Well, yaas—but—a—*essentially a Woman of the Nineteenth Century!*"

172　*30 April 1881*

flouting it. But once fashion has established itself as a universal force, accepted and obeyed by all but the very poorest, then to ensure that it is comfortable, practical and healthy becomes a matter of great moment; and deliberately to dress out of fashion is to become instantly conspicuous.

The dress of reform and the dress of protest are both inspired by the real or fancied shortcomings of contemporary fashion. In the former case the shortcomings are usually of a practical kind. Thus Elizabeth Cady Stanton first adopted bloomers because she found it difficult to walk upstairs in long skirts when holding a baby in her arms. In the latter case the grounds of complaint are often ideological – the feminists of the 1970s who wore combat dress did so not because it was the most practical clothing for the lives they led, but because it was a visible rejection of stereotyped femininity and matched their aggressive mood.

By the last quarter of the nineteenth century fashion had reached all but the very poorest classes of society. Stylish clothes could be produced to suit every pocket, and news of them could be quickly and efficiently disseminated through numerous fashion magazines. The middle classes might be outraged by their servants' ability to follow the fashions, but they were powerless to do anything about it. The fashions

TRUE ARTISTIC REFINEMENT.

" Died of a colour, in æsthetic pain."

Hostess. "WE'RE GOING DOWN TO SUPPER, MR. MIRABEL. LET ME INTRODUCE YOU TO MISS CHALMERS."

Mr. Mirabel. "A—PARDON ME—IS THAT THE TALL YOUNG LADY STANDING BY YOUR HUSBAND?"

Hostess. "YES. SHE'S THE MOST CHARMING GIRL I KNOW."

Mr. Mirabel. "I'VE NO DOUBT. BUT—A—SHE AFFECTS ANILINE DYES, DON'T YOU KNOW? I WEALLY COULDN'T GO DOWN TO SUPPAH WITH A YOUNG LADY WHO WEARS MAUVE TWIMMINGS IN HER SKIRT, AND MAGENTA WIBBONS IN HER HAIR!"

173 *17 February 1877*

themselves were more startling than becoming. The discovery of aniline dyes had ousted the gentle, muted shades of the early part of the century in favour of harsh pinks and acid yellows, unkind to all but the most perfect complexions, and the natural lines of the body were obliterated, first by a relentless pre-moulded corset, and second by the elaborately sculptured draperies which were built on to it. Asymmetry was the order of the day: a fashionable feature of the mid-1870s was a train 'à la boiteuse' – limping. And although this referred to the fact that one side was cut rounded and the other square, it also summed up the extraordinary impracticality of dresses at this time. Added to the crippling effect of the trained skirts was the sheer weight of the costume, most of which dragged on the waist.

Here were ideal conditions and ample provocation for movements of reform and protest. Reform was sought in the name of health and practicality. The 1880s saw the beginning of a very widespread interest in hygiene. The German Dr Jaeger was a pioneer in this field; he emphasized the need for healthy perspiration and popularized woollen and absorbent underwear. Beauty books of this time stress the importance of health and hygiene, and advocate plenty of exercise and unconstricted clothing. The Rational Dress Society, under Lady

Harberton, attempted to apply these principles to contemporary costume. Among other things she advocated divided skirts, which captured the public imagination more than any other item on her agenda, and prevented her from being taken very seriously. It was not for another decade or more that the tight grip of corsets, which were the prime offenders against health, was relaxed. On the whole the public opposed Rational Dress, insisting that reason and femininity were antithetical:

THE RATIONAL DRESS SHOW

In the Hall of the Prince is a Show – stuff and chintzes –
    (O Maidens of England, pray list to my song!)
For all there displayed is a warning that Ladies,
    In matters of dressing, are terribly wrong!
I thought my new bonnet, with roses upon it,
    And tasteful costume, was complete, I confess;
But now I'm reminded my eyes have been blinded
    To all the requirements of Rational Dress! . . .

See gowns hygienic, and frocks calisthenic,
    And dresses quite worthy a modern burlesque;
With garments for walking, and tennis, and talking,
    All terribly manful and too trouseresque!

174 *21 September 1878*

Y⁰ ÆSTHETIC young Geniuses!...

Y⁰ GORGEOUS young SWELLS!–

And habits for riding, for skating, or sliding,
  With 'rational' features they claim to possess;
The thought I can't banish, they're somewhat *too* mannish,
  And not quite the thing for a Rational Dress! . . .

'Tis hardy and boyish, not girlful and coyish –
  We think, as we stroll round the gaily-dight room –
A masculine coldness, a brusqueness, a boldness,
  Appears to pervade all this novel costume!
In ribbons and laces, and feminine graces,
  And soft flowing robes, there's a charm more or less –
I don't think I'll venture on dual garmenture,
  I fancy my own is the Rational Dress!

                                        2 June 1883

The dress reformers of the nineteenth century accepted as inevitable the attention they attracted. They knew that they often appeared ludicrous to the world at large, and they endured seeing their proposals ridiculed in the hope that one day their common sense would be recognized. But they did not set out to be conspicuous: the Bloomerites, for example, breathed private sighs of relief on returning to unobtrusive costume. This was not the case with the Aesthetes, who predated the Rational Dress movement by several years and were the first genuine protest-dressers.

The Aesthetes did not attempt to reform or modify contemporary dress: they rejected it outright. Their protest was both practical and ideological. Rebelling against the ugliness and shoddiness of Victorian industrial society, the essential article of their faith was that everything modern was horrible and that everything old was fine and noble (Plate 172). The women modelled themselves on the paintings of the old masters, which they admired in their then uncleaned state; eschewing the strident colours of their own day, they opted for sage green, dull crimson or soft blue (Plate 173). Tight-lacing was abhorrent to them, more for its gracelessness than its unhealthiness, and their dresses fell in fluid draperies. The men stopped short of doublet and hose and adopted instead the French 'artistic' costume of some forty years earlier – knee-breeches, velvet jackets, soft collars and floppy ties, and broad-brimmed hats (Plate 174). These clothes were accompanied by a soulful expression and an interesting pallor, as prescribed by William Morris in his 'Praise of My Lady':

A Tale of Modern Art and Fashion.

175   *7 September 1878*

176   *9 April 1881*

AN IMPARTIAL STATEMENT IN BLACK AND WHITE.

ÆSTHETIC LADY AND WOMAN OF FASHION.   WOMAN OF FASHION AND ÆSTHETIC LADY.

My lady seems of ivory
Forehead, straight nose, and cheeks that be
Hollow'd a little mournfully.

The Aesthetic movement did not stop at dress, but expressed itself in art, interior decoration and even pastimes. In its satirical serial 'The Rise and Fall of the Jack Spratts', *Punch* described an Aesthetic household (Plate 175):

Jack Spratt and his wife are playing 'Cat's Cradle', the twins are revolving quaint conceits in their aesthetic little minds; the friends are fondly lute-playing, or poring over old myths, and musing sadly on the light of other days; what time SALLY the Cook is dishing up a cold roast capon. . . . Say, reader, is it not a fair, glad, gracious picture?

7 September 1878

The Spratts' costume is in accordance with their beliefs. They are invited to a society reception, owing to the success of one of Jack's paintings:

Well, the SPRATTS duly attended that 'small and early', attired in their very best. Mr Punch forgets what Mrs SPRATT's very best consisted of at this particular period of her career; but rather thinks it must have been a broidered wimple, surcinctured with a golden liripipe over a welted chaisel-smock of watchet sergedusoy, lined with shalloon, and edged with vair, or possibly ermine.

JACK SPRATT so far gave way to the conventionalities of modern life as to wear a gent's evening suit complete for three-seventeen-six (made to order by a suburban tailor for this special occasion), and put a smart peacock's feather in his button-hole. At the same time, in order to show how simple and unworldly he really was, he sported a watch-guard made of common pack-thread, and left his luxuriant locks untouched by the comb.

14 September 1878

The upshot of the evening is that the Spratts are taken up by the fashionable world, with disastrous results for Mrs Spratt's aestheticism:

Mrs SPRATT's deep-rooted dislike to the female dress of the present day did not last much longer than her life-long prejudice

ÆSTHETICS.

Daughter of the House. "BY THE WAY, MR. SMITH, MAY I HAVE YOUR KIND PERMISSION TO TAKE THIS OFF THE CABINET, AND PUT IT INSIDE? THE MODERN MASCULINE HAT *IS* SUCH A DEPLORABLY HIDEOUS OBJECT!"

177   *25 May 1889*

against the aristocracy. The very next morning after that small-and-early, she discarded the mediaeval garments she had hitherto worn with such disdain for the eccentricities of modern fashion, and put herself into the hands of the best dress-maker in town. She had always looked lovely in her quaint old-fashioned attire, although the irreverent outside world had been wont to smile thereat as she took her walks abroad; but oh! how far lovelier she looked in the latest Paris mode, with chamois-leather under-clothing, and tightly clinging skirts that showed her as she really was!

Ibid.

Whether Aesthetic dress was actually beautiful and becoming is impossible to assess. Few Aesthetes would have been as easily seduced from their principles as Mrs Spratt. Certainly they had a point in condemning the ugliness around them, and their muted colour schemes and fluid lines are more in accordance with modern taste than mainstream fashion of the 1870s and 1880s. Furthermore, because the movement borrowed fairly indiscriminately from any period or style, provided only that it was old, it allowed more individuality than mainstream fashion. On the other hand, many people could see no charm in it: one of its leading exponents was described by Vernon Lee as

MEN AND MANNERS. A STUDY IN COSTUME.

Interested Philistine (to friend, who has taken him to Bohemian gathering). "AND WHO'S THE HORSEY-LOOKING MAN WITH THE BIG CIGAR?"
Friend. "OH—HE'S GUSTAVUS BROWNE, THE ARTIST. YOU REMEMBER HIS 'SOUL TRIUMPHANT OVER EARTHLY LOVE' IN THE LAST R.A.?"
I. P. "REALLY, YOU SURPRISE ME! AND WHO'S THE OTHER ARTIST HE'S TALKING TO?"
Friend. "ARTIST! GOOD HEAVENS! HE'S NOT AN ARTIST! HE'S A RETIRED UMBRELLA-MAKER WHO BOUGHT THE 'SOUL TRIUMPHANT'!"

'a tall melancholy drooping creature like an aged lily . . . in a dress of scantily embroidered antimacassars'. Doubtless *Punch* hit the nail on the head with its typically pragmatic 'Impartial Statement in Black and White' (Plate 176).

The essential point about the Aesthetes, which differentiates them from dress reformers and establishes them as the first in a long line of 'alternative' dressers, is that they had no wish for the rest of the world to dress like them. Aesthetes felt themselves superior to everybody else in sensitivity and artistic feeling. Things which others took for granted could either raise them to heights of ecstasy or give them intolerable pain (Plate 177). Their clothes proclaimed their membership of an exclusive clique, and the very Philistines whom they reviled were in fact essential to them, for without an audience to impress and shock they could not function. This strong element of exhibitionism, which is the hallmark of all protest dress, was pinpointed by W.S. Gilbert in Bunthorne's song from *Patience*:

Though the Philistines may jostle, you will rank as an apostle
in the high aesthetic band,

If you walk down Piccadilly with a poppy or a lily
in your mediaeval hand.
And everyone will say, As you walk your flowery way,
'If he's content with a vegetable love which would certainly not suit *me*,
Why, what a most particularly pure young man this pure young man
                                                        must be!'

Although the Aesthetic movement itself was of fairly short
duration, its influence on dress lasted well into the present century,
among those who were, or wished to be thought, artistic (Plate 178). The
author's grandmother, as a student at the Slade around 1905, affected
long loose robes made of William Morris fabrics and an intense
expression, and made her reluctant fiancé part his hair in the middle.
She was only slightly dashed when an interesting friend of her brother's
inquired why all artistic young women wore dresses made like sacks.
The key protest group of the 1920s were the Bohemians, but they
evolved quite naturally from the Aesthetes, and the transitional phase is
clearly illustrated in a poem of 1921. A Bohemian man, 'shaggy,

179   *8 February 1922*

"I'm giving a little party on Friday afternoon. Hope to get some interesting people together. Of course don't bother to dress—er—just wear whatever you feel like."

unkempt and grim', complete with cape and brigand hat (once again a throwback, this time to the French theatrical costume of some thirty years earlier, epitomized by Toulouse-Lautrec's picture of Aristide Bruant), meets a Philistine girl at a party and they fall in love. She determines to make herself worthy of him:

> Home she went in a raptured daze,
> Looked in a mirror with startled gaze,
> Didn't seem to be pleased at all;
> Savagely muttered: 'Insipid Doll!'
> Clutched her hair and a pair of shears,
> Cropped and bobbed it behind the ears;
> Aimed at a wan and willowy-necked
> Sort of a Holman Hunt effect;
> Robed in subtile and sage-green tones,
> Like the dames of Rossetti and E.B. Jones;
> Girdled her garments billowing wide,
> Moved with an undulating glide;

180   *15 May 1929*

Chelsea Host. "Sorry, old man, I ought to have told you. We're quite alone—you needn't have bothered to dress yourself up."

> All her frivolous friends forsook,
> Cultivated a soulful look;
> Gushed in a voice with a creamy throb
> Over some weirdly Futurist daub –
> Did all, in short, that a woman can
> To be a consummate Bohemian.

Inevitably, when she meets him again, he too has changed. He has cut and combed his hair, acquired smart new clothes and become a man-about-town in order to be worthy of her, so that they are as far apart as ever.

Later on, Bohemian women abandoned Pre-Raphaelite models and developed their own style, but in their early years they still owed much to aestheticism. Augustus John, whose ideas on art and craftsmanship derived substantially from William Morris, insisted that they be given expression in the clothes of his household. Nicolette Devas has described just what this meant for the wearers:

> The older boys went to a local school dressed in long belted smocks over corduroy trousers and [with] their hair in long bobs. These clothes set them apart and in self-defence they became a gang of John boys against all comers. . . . Augustus found the fashions of the day unpaintable, and his household dressed to suit his painting. Dodo and Edie were skilled dressmakers and evolved the long flowing skirts gathered at the waist, and the loose smock top with the sleeves cut in one. . . . The John clothes did not stop at dresses, but probed deeper to underclothes. The girls suffered bitterly from the cold. For not only were stockings and closed knickers banished, but wool vests or combinations too. I shall never forget the horrible chilliness of draughty linen against the skin.

Bohemian men's dress was not all that different from Aesthetic dress, perhaps because the mainstream styles they were rebelling against did not change very much either. Both protest groups favoured soft collars and floppy neckties (the Bohemians also liking roll-neck jerseys), wide-brimmed hats and long hair, and soft-textured fabrics like velvet. Bohemians also favoured facial hair (Plate 179). Women's dress showed more variety. Just as the Aesthetes had drawn on any period for inspiration, provided it was long past, so Bohemians turned to a wide variety of ethnic sources. They might wear oriental trousers and shawls (Plate 180), or copy gipsy styles and colours (Plate 181), stress their

Waiter. "SHALL I TAKE YOUR HAT, SIR?"
True Bohemian. "NO, THANKS; I EAT OUT OF IT."

181   *24 April 1929*

masculine or feminine characteristics, provided only that the result was sufficiently unusual to attract attention. For the Bohemians carried their exhibitionism a stage further than the Aesthetes had done. Aesthetes were happy to mingle in conventional society; Bohemians preferred to gather in their own meeting-places (Plates 182 and 183). Aesthetes did not differ from other people in their manners or habits; Bohemians had a taste for the outrageous (see Plate 181). Aesthetes were unconcerned with politics and their private lives were conventional; Bohemians were strongly connected with socialism and free love. Instead of merely rejecting ugliness, Bohemians rejected the whole fabric of bourgeois society. The tie became the symbol of all they despised, and was duly spurned (Plate 184). Not surprisingly, *Punch* remained unimpressed by the movement:

> In a mews behind Mulberry Square
>> Was the party to which I was called;
> The men were all covered with hair
>> And the women were more or less bald;
> With her feet on a spongy divan
>> And the rest of herself on the floor
> I saw what I thought was a man,
>> But in fact was Banana the Bore –

BITTER BLOW TO BRIGHTER CHELSEA.

Old Lady from the country (who has been taken by nephew to famous Bohemian club). "I AM GRATIFIED TO DISCOVER, MY DEAR NOEL, THAT YOU FREQUENT A PLACE WHICH IS PATRONISED BY THE CLERGY."

Banana the High-brow, Banana the Bore,
With her feet on the sofa, her frame on the floor.
Young poets sat cross-legged and gaped in a row
At the Empress of Chelsea, Princess of Soho;
But I heard what I took for a delicate snore
From the Queen of the High-brows, Banana the Bore.

Her clothes had come over the seas
   From Russia, the Riff or the Rhine,
Her dress was a nightie (Chinese)
   And her shoes of a Spanish design;
She woke and she eyed me askance,
   She hummed an Italian air,
Then sighed that her soul was in France,
   And I wished that her body was there . . .

Banana, Banana sits mum as a cat;
They say she is deep, and perhaps it is that.
She hasn't much use for the men of her race,
But dig up a Dago and watch the girl's face!
She doesn't like me, as I've hinted before,
And I can't say I dote on Banana the Bore.

21 April 1926

A HERD OF WILD BOHEMIANS BEING ROUNDED UP FOR THE OPENING OF A NEW CAFÉ IN SOHO, WITH THE IDEA OF CREATING THE RIGHT ATMOSPHERE.

By the 1930s, the Aesthetic ideal of fine craftsmanship and abhorrence of mass production had become diluted and vulgarized, via the ethnic cults of the Bohemians, into mere arty-craftiness. It was satirized by Stella Gibbons in the character of Elfine, whom Flora Poste besought to avoid 'orange linen jumpers and hand-wrought jewellery. Oh, and shawls in the evening', and no less sharply by *Punch*:

> I'd love to go all warp and woof and weft,
>   All loomy, peasant-weavey, folk-designy,
> And wear my hair dead straight and dress all Left,
>   But ... well, I *so* adore things smooth and shiny;
>   I'm weak – I fall for textiles which
>   Don't itch.
>
> I'd love to go all adze and gouge (or googe?),
>   All feeling-for-material, way-of-grainy;
> Perhaps I'm just a mass-production stooge,
>   But woodwork 'lightly-waxed-of-*course*-no-stainy'
>   Looks sort of, you know, prototype –
>   Unripe.

I'd love to go all leather-craft, with thongs,
   Hand-tooly, suedy, floppy and embossy,
Dark purple 'Igor Plotsky – Seven Songs' –
    But then the things in shops are firm and glossy,
      And kind of leathery *both* sides –
        Not hides.

I'd love to go all underglaze and slip –
   It's so divinely squeezable and squishy –
All torso-without-arms (the arms *do* chip),
    And beakery and ewery and dishy . . .
      But aren't they always, somehow, *thick* –
        Like brick?

I'd love to go all dress-length, make-my-own,
   Just-nipped-in-at-the-waist and *rather* flowing,
But why do they always look, well, overblown,
    As if they'd left a lot of room for growing?
      I want to sort of feel I've dressed,
        Not guessed.

I'd love to go – I *am*, deep-down inside –
   All self-expressy and creative-urgey;
It's the results I can't seem to abide.
    I know I'm wrong – it's some sort of allergy –
      But every time my verdict goes
        To pros.

                            7th July 1948

Thus by the end of the 1940s the dress of protest had cut loose from the concept of art, though it might still cling to vaguely intellectual associations. But, for the post-Hiroshima Bohemians and later beatniks, the primary rebellion was a political one. Aesthetic considerations were dwarfed into insignificance by the prospect of total extinction, and the protest dressers of the 1950s aimed at a complete disregard for their appearance, which ranged from mere scruffiness (Plate 185) to actual dirt (Plate 186). But despite the sense of doom and futility engendered by the threat of the bomb, in many respects the post-war Bohemians differed little from their pre-war counterparts. In the late 1950s *Punch* serialized a survey of London life inspired by Mayhew's research a century earlier, which was carried out by Alex Atkinson and Ronald Searle. One of the instalments is devoted to a Bohemian soirée which

"HEARD OF ANYONE CALLED BARCHESTER-CHOLMONDELY-SMYTHE HERE? SWINE WEARS A TIE."

184   *17 March 1937*

185   *3 May 1961*
186   *25 January 1961*

"Sis won't be long—she's mussing her hair."

*"If we're not careful, not only are we going to get
soaked but clean as well."*

Atkinson managed to infiltrate, 'having been introduced into the circle
as a temporary sub-editor on a periodical devoted to gardening'. The
other guests have equally tenuous connections with the world of culture.
In the expanded book of the survey, which appeared soon after,
Atkinson adds that 'my disguise consisted of a woollen "sweater", a
tobogganing cap, and a copy of the *New Statesman*'. Although the
evening described (Plate 187) is tame enough, it is clear that the
participants imagine themselves to be not only intellectual but morally
and socially emancipated, a direct legacy of pre-war bohemianism:

> That they were fully aware of the dissolute nature of their
> behaviour, and revelled in it, I was left in no doubt; for their
> laughter was shrill and uninhibited. Here, out of the sight of
> ordinary conventional citizens, they could shamelessly loosen their
> neckties, comb their hair in full view of the company, take vodka
> and sherry wine in the same glass, exhibit their legs to above the
> knee if they were females, audaciously belittle the reputations of
> eminent personages, throw cigarette-ends out of the window, and
> stay awake until long after the normal hour for retiring: and all
> without any qualm of conscience or thought for the morrow.
>
> 5 February 1958

The 1950s were also characterized by youthful rebellion against the
older generation. Tension has always existed between parents and
children; now it was crystallized in the cult film *Rebel without a Cause*
(1955), in the music of Elvis Presley and Bill Haley (one need only think
back to the nervousness with which cinema managers showed *Rock
around the Clock* (1956) to realize how threatening it seemed), in the
much-reported exploits of the Teddy boys, and in a new style of
masculine dress borrowed from America, and later Italy, which was
arrogant, sexy and defiant. This was not a political protest, except in so
far as it was provoked by the drabness and austerity of the post-war
world, nor an economic one – James Dean's rebel came from a
comfortable middle-class home. It was a rejection of the banality, the
uniformity and the lack of excitement of adult life and its responsibilities.
Because young people were not yet the prestigious economic group that
they were to become in the next decade, their revolt took the form of a
spare-time activity, to be fitted in between less glamorous pursuits:

The new Mayhew—a Bohemian soirée in the Metropolis

187   *5 February 1958*

"Protest clothes on the second floor sir."

188   *7 June 1967*

THE HEP-CAT'S LAMENT

I loved the way he wore his jazzy tie,
His pointed winkle-picker suedette shoes,
His well-set hair that showed a bronzy dye,
His mellow voice, forever crooning blues.

I'd find him in the snack-bar every night,
With cup in hand and cigarette on lip,
The juke-box trembled, playing 'Travelling Light',
He'd tap a foot, rotate a lazy hip.

Gone are his tight Italian pin-striped jeans,
Gone are his side-burns, grown with anxious care,
He's left the juke-box to the older teens,
I loved him once, but now I'm in despair.

Grey billowing flannels now conform to rule,
He's back in Prefect's uniform, at school.

3 May 1961

Throughout the 1960s the teenage sector advanced as rapidly in earning power as it did in social emancipation. Youth fashion became a hugely lucrative industry and ceased to spell protest. Denim, for example, which when worn by Dean or Presley had epitomized rebellion, became defused by over-exposure and ended up simply run-of-the-mill. Protest dress was no longer primarily inspired by the generation gap, although by now it was largely restricted to the young. In the second half of the 1960s it found its chief impetus in the Vietnam War. The effect of that war was felt in many ways. Protest became a marketable commodity, and singers like Joan Baez and Bob Dylan, and hosts of imitators, poured out songs about man's inhumanity to man. Marches and demonstrations were undertaken, and the clothes worn by the protesters amounted to a kind of uniform (Plate 188). Parallel to this

189   *3 June 1981*

"I shouldn't worry. They'll grow out of it."

"*In the Fifties I was a Bohemian, in the Sixties I was a beatnik and in the Seventies I was a hippy but now I'm just middle-class.*"

Xan Pyne

190 *16 December 1981*

direct response can be placed the derisive adoption of army and other uniforms, which, when combined with long hair and the androgynous appearance of the time, ridiculed traditional militaristic attitudes and represented a flouting of authority in general. But perhaps most important of all was the hippie phenomenon. In defiance of the aggression, restless materialism and snappy, functional clothes of their age, hippies promoted peace and mysticism, wearing long hair and flowing robes, accompanied by flowers, bells and drugs. Like the Aesthetes, they chose to opt out rather than to reform, but instead of looking to the past they sought their inspiration from the East. However naïve, superficial and even 'pseud' they may have been, they had a profound influence on middle-class life-style and paved the way for the ethnic fashions of the 1970s. But their proclaimed millennium was overtaken by world recession, which threw up its own brand of protest. The astonished flower children found that they had spawned the cynical punk generation, ostentatiously flouting good manners, good taste and their parents' pacifist values (Plate 189).

The last few years have seen what amounts to the most triumphant, though largely unrecognized, dress of protest yet to appear. Ever since fashion began, it has been used to advertise wealth and social status, with people spending all they could afford, and more, on blatantly expensive clothes. Conspicuous expenditure has been one of its constant elements. In our own age of mass unemployment, particularly among the most fashion-conscious age-group, this is no longer a viable concern. It has therefore been quite substantially rejected in favour of what we might call conspicuous thrift. Clothes are unearthed at jumble sales and in charity shops, and a good find is as much an occasion for pride as an expensive purchase used to be. The clothes are worn with much creative imagination, so that anything can be turned to good account. Even clothes bought in regular shops conform to this ideal. Grandad shirts and oversized trousers held up by a belt slotted through dropped carriers are examples of fashions which deliberately emulate jumble-sale booty. The emphasis on personal interpretation and the rejection of the traditional economic symbolism of dress constitute the truly original protest dress of our age, and it is the only one possible in a society where all styles of dress are acceptable, all extremes of behaviour are permissible and protest itself has become fully integrated into daily life (Plate 190).

References

Introduction
Susan and Asa Briggs, *Cap and Bell*. London: Macdonald, 1972, Preface.

1 Domestic Bliss
Charles Dickens, *Sketches by Boz*. London, 1836, 'The Mistaken Milliner'.
Daphne du Maurier, *Rebecca*. London: Gollancz, 1938.
Sonia Keppel, *Edwardian Daughter*. London: Hamish Hamilton, 1958, ch. 9.
The Brothers Mayhew, *The Greatest Plague of Life*. London, 1847; quoted in E. Royston
     Pike (ed.), *Human Documents of the Victorian Golden Age*. London: Allen & Unwin, 1967.
Samuel Richardson, *Pamela*. London, 1740, Letters VI and VII.
George R. Sims, *Mary Jane's Memoirs*. London: Chatto & Windus, 1887, Memoir I.
Tobias Smollett, *Humphry Clinker*. London, 1771; Everyman edn, London: Dent, 1965,
     p. 199.
Flora Thompson, *Lark Rise to Candleford*. Harmondsworth, Middx: Penguin, 1973,
     ch. 10.

2 The Venus of Milo
Michael Arlen, *The Green Hat*. London: Collins, 1924, ch. 1.
F. Scott Fitzgerald, *The Great Gatsby*. London: Chatto & Windus, 1926, chs 1 and 3.
Brigid Keenan, *Dior in Vogue*. London: Octopus, 1981, ch. 2.
Gwen Raverat, *Period Piece*. London: Faber & Faber, 1952, ch. 13.
Sarah Tytler, *Girl Neighbours*. Glasgow: Blackie, *c.* 1885, ch. 1.

3 The Poetry of Motion
Sonia Keppel, *Edwardian Daughter*, ch. 2.
Gwen Raverat, *Period Piece*, ch. 13.
Laura Ingalls Wilder, *Little Town on the Prairie*. London: Lutterworth, 1963, ch. 23.

4 New Bits to Show
Dorothy Canfield, *The Bent Twig*. London: Constable, 1923, Bk II, ch. 19.
Edna Woolman Chase, *Always in Vogue*. London: Gollancz, 1954, ch. 16.
George Eliot, *The Mill on the Floss*. London, 1860, Bk VI, ch. 10.
John Galsworthy, *The Silver Spoon*. London: Heinemann, 1926, ch. 4.
Sonia Keppel, *Edwardian Daughter*, ch. 14.

5 The Way to Wareham
William Caxton, *The Book of the Knight of the Tower*. Oxford: Early English Text Society,
     1971, ch. 42.
Charles Nielsen Gatty, *The Bloomer Girls*. Las Vegas, Nev.: Femina, 1967, *passim*.

6 Trinity or Girton?
John Galsworthy, *The Silver Spoon*, ch. 4.
Eric Gill, *Clothes*. London: Jonathan Cape, 1931, ch. 8.
Fraser Harrison, *The Dark Angel*. London: Sheldon Press, 1977, ch. 7.
Anita Loos, *A Girl Like I*. London: Hamish Hamilton, 1967, ch. 7.

7 Seaside Costumes

Charles Dickens, *Sketches by Boz*, 'The Tuggses at Ramsgate'.

Francis Kilvert, *Diary*, ed. William Plomer. London: Jonathan Cape, 3 vols, 1938–40; repr. 1961; Vol. 3, entries for 12 June 1874 and 13 July 1875.

Christopher Marsden, *The English at the Seaside*. London: Collins, 1947, *passim*.

Gwen Raverat, *Period Piece*, ch. 6.

8 Protest Clothes

Alex Atkinson and Ronald Searle, *The Big City*. London: Perpetua, 1958, 'A Bohemian Soirée in the Metropolis'.

Stella Blum, *Victorian Fashions and Costumes from Harper's Bazaar*. New York: Dover, 1974, ch. 2.

Nicolette Devas, *Two Flamboyant Fathers*. London: Collins, 1966, ch. 3.

Stella Gibbons, *Cold Comfort Farm*. London: Longman, 1932, ch. 11.

W.S. Gilbert, *Patience*, 1881.

Leonée Ormond, 'Female Costume in the Aesthetic Movement of the 1870s and 1880s', in *Costume* (1967–8).

Robert W. Service, *Ballads of a Bohemian*. London: T. Fisher Unwin, 1921, 'The Philistine and the Bohemian'.